Praise for *Baby-Led Weaning*

"[Rapley and Murkett] encourage parents to forgo the usual baby purée and move straight to whole foods while continuing to breastfeed primarily after a baby is six months old. Their arguments are scientifically sound, especially when it comes to muscle development in the mouth, and they address the anticipated counterarguments. . . . If mine were little again, I would definitely try this. As long as mom is nursing, who says baby can't eat lamb chops?"   —*Library Journal*, starred review

"I've been telling mothers for years that when babies start grabbing food from the table, they are ready for solids. I had the pleasure of observing this with my own children. What I love about this book is the joy and zest the authors put into parenting, their commonsense approach, and their faith that babies will do the right things for themselves when the time is right. Baby-led weaning is easy, and it makes parenting fun!"

—Nikki Lee, RN, MS, IBCLC

"It sounds like common sense: After all, would you want to be strapped into a high chair and force-fed spoon after spoon of bland vegetables? It's surely much more exciting to be able to exercise a bit of control over your diet."   —*The Guardian*

"The benefits are great."   —*Independent*

"[Baby-led weaning] makes life so much easier."

—*The Times* (London)

THE EXPERIMENT

BECAUSE EVERY BOOK IS A TEST OF NEW IDEAS

"I see many happy children, who choose their own food independently and eat at their own pace."

—STEPHAN KLEINTJES, pediatric dietitian

"It's been wonderful, and very funny, watching her discover food, her great concentration in navigating new textures and exploring new tastes. . . . One of our favorite things about baby-led weaning is its emphasis on families eating together."

—NICOLA KENT, *The Guardian*

"The thing I really love about baby-led weaning is that my son can actively participate in family meals. . . . I love that I don't have to cook two different meals, I simply have to adjust our family meal to ensure it's suitable for him. . . . We're having a blast watching our little man truly learn to enjoy and appreciate food in all of its glory. And it's so much easier than purées!"

—naturalparentingtips.com

"Sharing food with Mirah has turned out to be one of the great joys of parenting. Watching her respond to the pleasures of ripe tomatoes, curried rice noodles, and all kinds of meats and vegetables has made mealtime a much more enjoyable experience for all three of us. We can tell she is learning through all of her senses about how various substances respond to being crumbled or dropped or mushed. She seems to really like that she is eating the same foods as we are, and since we are generally sharing the same meal, I am more likely to make us all something healthy."   —AIMEE POHL, babble.com

"You just hand them the food in a suitably sized piece and if they like it they eat it and if they don't they won't. . . . That's the essence of baby-led weaning. No purees, no ice cube trays, no food processor, no potato masher . . . just you and your child, eating food that you enjoy with you and your family. . . . I can't even begin to tell you how pleasant it is to eat in a restaurant with your baby-led weaning child chomping on a piece of bread and butter or a chunk of cucumber from your salad beside you."   —Aitch, babyledweaning.blogware.com

Baby-Led Weaning

Also by Gill Rapley and Tracey Murkett

The Baby-Led Weaning Cookbook: 130 Easy, Nutritious Recipes That Will Help Your Baby Learn to Eat (and Love!) a Variety of Solid Foods—and That the Whole Family Will Enjoy

Baby-Led Breastfeeding: Follow Your Baby's Instincts for Relaxed and Easy Nursing

Baby-Led Weaning

The Essential Guide to
Introducing Solid Foods
and Helping Your Baby to Grow Up a
Happy and Confident Eater

GILL RAPLEY and TRACEY MURKETT

THE EXPERIMENT
New York

BABY-LED WEANING: *The Essential Guide to Introducing Solid Foods—and Helping Your Baby to Grow Up a Happy and Confident Eater*

The Experiment, LLC
220 East 23rd Street, Suite 301
New York, NY 10010–4674
www.theexperimentpublishing.com

Originally published in the United Kingdom in 2008 by Vermilion, an imprint of Ebury Publishing/Random House Group. This edition, which has been adapted and revised for North America, is published by arrangement with Vermilion.

This book is a work of nonfiction. Some of the names of people in the case studies have been changed solely to protect the privacy of others.

Many of the designations used by manufacturers and sellers to distinguish their products are claimed as trademarks. Where those designations appear in this book and The Experiment was aware of a trademark claim, the designations have been capitalized.

Library of Congress Control Number: 2010924688

ISBN 978-1-61519-021-8
Ebook ISBN 978-1-61519-124-6

Cover design by Alison Forner
Front cover photograph courtesy of Janice Milnerwood
Text design by Neuwirth & Associates, Inc.

Manufactured in the United States of America

First published October 2010

Distributed by Workman Publishing Company, Inc.
Distributed simultaneously in Canada by Thomas Allen & Son Limited

20 19 18 17 16 15 14 13 12

Contents

Preface

BABY-LED WEANING WAS around long before the first edition of this book became available; we certainly didn't invent the idea that babies will naturally feed themselves when they are ready! And yet for many years, most parents, understandably so, have assumed that babies need to be spoon-fed, with few of us realizing we could let our baby feed himself right from the start. After working for many years as a public health nurse, and having her own children, Gill became curious about self-feeding among babies, which led to her research on the topic. She called the idea baby-led weaning, and conference talks and press articles soon followed. Tracey, a freelance writer, heard about baby-led weaning and was inspired to try the approach with her own daughter. She contacted Gill to find out more about baby-led weaning, with the aim of writing a magazine article about it—instead we decided to write this book.

Since the publication of *Baby-Led Weaning*, we've both enjoyed seeing more and more parents adopt the approach and have been amazed how quickly the idea has traveled across the globe, first through word of mouth and then through the Internet, which continues to carry stories, photos, and videos of babies self-feeding. Parents have seen how well babies and toddlers eat when they are allowed to feed themselves, and many have realized with a sigh of relief that they don't need to struggle with spoon-feeding their child after all. By letting their baby take the lead, they can avoid the mealtime problems that we all thought were an inevitable part of raising kids.

You'll now find baby-led weaning (or baby-led solids as it's sometimes known) featured on almost every parenting Web site, with lively discussions in forums and chat rooms. Since this book first appeared, it has been translated into several languages, and health professionals the world over are beginning to recommend the baby-led concept to parents as a way to reduce the stress of introducing solids and help their children enjoy good food.

As parents ourselves, we are delighted to think that our book might help you and your little one enjoy the wonderful journey that self-feeding can be. If you have a baby—or are planning to have one—read on!

Gill Rapley & Tracey Murkett
Summer 2010

Introduction

THE FIRST TIME a baby eats solid food is a milestone for any parent—it's a new chapter in a baby's life, and it's exciting. And as he takes his first mouthful of food parents cross their fingers and hope that their child will be a "good eater." They want him to enjoy food, to eat healthily, and they want to have easy, stress-free family mealtimes.

But many parents find the first few years of solid food are not much fun for either them or their child. They struggle with common problems, whether it's getting their baby to accept lumpy food, or coping with picky eating or mealtime battles with a toddler. Often families settle for separate mealtimes and different food for adults and children.

Most babies start their journey to grown-up eating by being spoon-fed their first mouthfuls of puréed food on a date decided by their parents. But what happens if you don't do it like this? What happens if you let your baby decide when and how to start solids? What happens if you let him handle "real" food himself instead of spoon-feeding him? In other words, what happens if you let your baby lead the way?

Well, like many families, you and your baby will almost certainly find the whole adventure more fun. He'll show you when he's ready to start, and he'll share your meals from the very beginning. He'll learn about healthy family food by tasting and testing it and by feeding himself—no mush or purées but real food. And he'll be able to do all this from about six months onward.

Baby-led weaning (BLW) will develop your baby's chewing skills, manual dexterity, and hand-eye coordination. With your help, he'll discover a wide range of healthy foods and learn important social skills. And he'll eat only as much as he needs, which may make him less likely to be overweight when he is older. Most of all, he'll enjoy it—and he'll almost certainly be happy and confident at mealtimes as a result.

Baby-led weaning is safe, natural, and easy—and, like most good ideas in parenting, it's not new. Parents the world over have discovered it for themselves, simply by watching their babies. Baby-led weaning works whether your baby is breast-fed, formula-fed, or having a mixture of the two. And, according to parents who have tried both BLW and spoon-feeding, letting your baby lead the way is much easier and more enjoyable all around.

Of course, there's nothing revolutionary about giving babies finger foods starting at six months. What's different about BLW is that the baby has *only* finger foods, making purées and spoon-feeding a thing of the past.

This book will show you why BLW is the logical way to introduce solids and why trusting your baby's skills and instincts makes sense. It will provide you with practical tips for getting started and the low-down on what to expect. It will let you in on one of the best-kept secrets of stress-free parenting.

With BLW there's no program to follow and no stages to complete. Your baby won't have to work his way through a series of smooth purées, mashed food, and lumpy meals before he's allowed to eat "real" food—and you won't have to follow a complicated daily timetable of meals. Instead you'll be able to relax and enjoy your baby's adventures with food.

Most books on introducing solids contain recipes and menu planners; this book is different. It's more about *how* to let your baby feed himself rather than *what* to offer him. Planning "baby meals" assumes that babies can't have ordinary family food or that their food has to be prepared separately. But most meals in any healthy cookbook can be adapted easily so that your six-month-old baby can share them. As long as your own diet is healthy and nutritious there's no need for separate recipes.

We have, however, included some suggestions for good first foods and foods to avoid to help you get started. And, because many parents see BLW as an opportunity to look at what *they* eat, we've provided guidelines on how to ensure a healthy and balanced diet for the whole family. If you've been living on junk food or prepackaged meals, you can use this book to help you turn over a new leaf.

Baby-led weaning can be great fun for you and your baby. If you haven't seen any other babies start solids this way, you'll probably be amazed at how quickly your baby becomes skilled at handling different foods and how adventurous he is with new tastes compared with other children. Babies are *happier* doing things for themselves—and it helps them learn.

Many parents who have used a baby-led approach have shared their experiences with us. Some had found spoon-feeding difficult in the past; others had turned to BLW in frustration when their six-month-old refused to be spoon-fed. Some were first-time parents who were attracted by BLW's reputation as a gentle and commonsense way to introduce solids. What we heard time and time again was that their babies absolutely loved it, and that they became—and remained—happy and sociable eaters.

We hope this book will help you to discover just how easy the transition to family meals can be and how using a baby-led approach can provide the foundation for a lifetime of healthy, enjoyable eating for your baby.

Note: Throughout this book we've tried to be fair to boys and girls by alternating "he" and "she," chapter by chapter. No difference between boys and girls is implied.

1.

What is Baby-Led Weaning?

"For most parents mealtimes seem to be a nightmare. With Emily that's one major battle we just don't have to face. We really enjoy mealtimes. Food is not an issue at all."
Jess, mother of Emily, 2

"It's so much easier to introduce the same food that everyone else is eating. I just don't worry about whether or not Ben will eat something the way I did with the others when I was spoon-feeding. This feels so natural—and so much more enjoyable."
Sam, mother of Bella, 8, Alex, 5, and Ben, 8 months

What is Weaning?

Weaning is the gradual change that a baby makes from having breast milk or formula as her only food to having no breast milk or formula at all. This changeover takes *at least* six months but may—especially with breast-feeding—last several years. This book is about the beginning of the weaning process, which starts with the baby's very first mouthful of solid food.*

These first solids—sometimes called complementary foods—are not meant to take over from breast milk or formula but to add to (or "complement") it, so that the baby's diet gradually becomes more varied.

In most families, weaning is led by the parents. When they start to spoon-feed their baby, they are deciding when and how she starts solids; when they stop offering the breast or bottle they are deciding when to end milk feedings. You could call it parent-led weaning. Baby-led weaning (BLW) is different. It allows the baby to lead the whole process, using her instincts and abilities. She determines when weaning should start and finish. Although this may sound odd, it makes perfect sense when you look closely at how babies develop.

Why BLW is Different

When people think about introducing a baby's first solid foods, they usually picture an adult with a spoon and a few teaspoonfuls of puréed carrot or apple. Sometimes the baby will open her mouth eagerly to take the spoon—but she is just as likely to spit the food out, push the spoon away, cry or refuse to eat. Many parents resort to games—"Here comes the train!"—in an effort to persuade the baby to accept food, which is often different from the family meals and given at a different time.

In the Western world this approach to feeding babies is very rarely questioned, and most people take it for granted

---

*Throughout this book, "weaning" refers to the introduction of solid foods. However, the term "weaning" can also be used to describe the transition from breast milk to formula. For this reason, baby-led weaning is sometimes also called "baby-led solids."

that spoon-feeding is the normal way to go about weaning. And yet dictionary definitions for spoon-feeding include: "to provide (someone) with so much help or information that they do not need to think for themselves"[1] and "to treat (another) in a way that discourages independent thought or action."[2] Baby-led weaning, by contrast, encourages a baby's confidence and independence by following *her* cues. Solid feeding starts when the baby demonstrates that she can feed herself and progresses at her unique pace. It allows her to follow her instincts to copy her parents and her brothers and sisters and to develop her feeding skills in a natural, fun way, learning as she goes.

If they are given the chance, almost all babies will show their parents that they are ready for something other than milk simply by grabbing a piece of food and taking it to their mouths. They don't need their parents to decide when weaning should start and they don't need to be spoon-fed; babies can do it themselves.

This is what happens in BLW:

- The baby sits with the rest of the family at mealtimes, and joins in when she is ready.
- She is encouraged to explore food as soon as she is interested, by picking it up with her hands—it doesn't matter whether or not she manages to eat any at first.
- Food is offered in pieces that are the size and shape that the baby can handle easily, rather than as purées or mashed food.
- She *feeds herself* from the start, rather than being spoon-fed by someone else.
- It's up to the baby how much she eats, and how quickly she widens the range of foods she enjoys.

- The baby continues to have milk feedings (breast milk or formula) whenever she wants them and she decides when she is ready to begin reducing them.

The first experiences of eating solid food can have an impact on the way a baby feels about mealtimes for many years, so it makes sense to make them enjoyable. But weaning for many babies—and their parents—isn't much fun. Of course, not *all* babies mind being spoon-fed in the conventional way, but many appear to resign themselves to it rather than truly enjoy it. On the other hand, babies who are allowed to feed themselves and eat with the family seem to love mealtimes.

> "When Ryan was about six months I went out with a group of moms with babies the same age. The mothers were busy spooning purée into their babies and wiping around their mouths with the spoon, making sure every bit went in. They seemed to be making their lives so hard, and you could see the babies weren't enjoying it."
>
> Suzanne, mother of Ryan, 2

Why BLW Makes Sense

Babies and children crawl, walk, and talk when they are ready. These developmental milestones won't happen any sooner and—*provided babies are given the opportunity*—they won't happen any later than the right time for that baby. When you put your newborn on the floor to kick her legs, you are giving her the opportunity to roll over. When she can, she will. You're also providing her with the opportunity to get up and walk. That may take a bit longer. Keep on providing the opportunity and she will do it eventually. Why should feeding be any different?

Healthy babies are able to feed themselves from their mother's breast as soon as they are born. By the time they are about six months old they are able to reach out and grab pieces of food and take them to their mouths. We've always known that they can do this and, for many years, parents have been encouraged to introduce finger foods at around six months. But there is now evidence to suggest that babies shouldn't be having *any* solids before this age (see below). Since babies can begin to feed themselves with finger foods starting at six months, there seems to be no need for puréed foods at all.

However, even though we now know that babies have both the instinct and the ability to feed themselves at the right time, spoon-feeding is still the way most babies are fed during their first year—and sometimes for much longer.

When Should a Baby Start Solids?

The World Health Organization (and many other authorities, such as Health Canada and the UK Departments of Health) currently recommends that all babies should be gradually introduced to solid foods at around six months.[3] At the time of this writing, the advice from the American Academy of Pediatrics is less clear: It says that most babies are ready to start solids between four and six months but adds that they should be able to sit up by themselves and grab things to take to their mouths. Most babies cannot do this until they are about six months old. Evidence suggests that giving solids earlier than six months is not good for babies because:

- Solid foods are not as densely packed with nutrients and calories as breast milk or formula. Young babies have small tummies and need a concentrated, easily digestible source of calories and nutrients for healthy growth; only breast milk or formula can provide this.
- The baby's digestive system isn't able to get all the goodness out of solid foods, so they pass through her without giving her proper nourishment.
- If she has solids too early, the baby's appetite for breast milk or formula goes down, so she gets even less nourishment.
- Babies who are given solid foods early get more infections and are at greater risk of developing allergies than those who stay on breast milk or formula until six months, because their immune systems are immature.

Feeding babies solid foods earlier than six months has also been found to make them more prone to risk factors for heart disease in later life, such as high blood pressure.

Knowing when to start solids

♦ *False signs of readiness*

Over the years parents have been told to watch out for a variety of signs to help them figure out when their baby is ready for solid food. Most are just part of normal development, linked to the baby's age, not to her readiness for other foods. And there are some other "signs of readiness" that are equally unreliable as guides to starting solids, yet are still thought by many people to show that something more than milk is needed:

■ *Waking at night.* Many parents start solids early in the hope that this will help their baby to sleep through the night. They assume that she is waking because she is hungry; but babies wake at night for all sorts of reasons, and there is no evidence that giving them solids solves the problem. If they *are* genuinely hungry, babies under six months need to be offered more breast milk (or formula, if they are formula-fed), not solids.

■ *Weight gain slowing slightly.* This is a common reason for parents to be advised to start solids early, but research has shown this is something that normally happens at around four months, especially in breast-fed babies.[4] It's not a sign that they need solids.

■ *Watching their parents eat.* From about four months babies are fascinated by everyday family activities, such as dressing, shaving, and eating. But they don't understand what these things mean—they're just curious.

■ *Making lip-smacking noises.* Babies who are learning how to use their mouths enjoy practicing these skills, which are as much about learning to talk as they are about eating. They're part of a baby's early preparation for solid foods but they don't mean she's ready to start.

■ *Not going straight to sleep after milk feedings.* Babies of about four months are more alert and wakeful than younger babies; they simply need less sleep.

■ *Small baby.* When babies are small it's either because they are meant to be small or because they need more nourishment. If they are under six months, it's breast milk or formula they need to help them "catch up," not solids. The exception to this is babies who are born very prematurely, some of whom may need extra nutrients earlier than six months (see page 57).

■ *Big baby.* Babies who are born big (or who get big very quickly) don't need extra food. They are big either because of their genetic makeup or, in some cases (especially if they are formula-fed), because they are already having more milk than they really need. Their digestive and immune systems are no more mature than any other babies', so the health risks of giving solids early are just the same. The idea that big babies need food earlier is left over from the 1950s and 1960s, when it was mistakenly believed that once a baby reached a certain weight (commonly 12 lbs), she needed solid foods. Milk is all a baby needs for the first six months—however big or small she is. *Size doesn't matter.*

> "I've never understood why people say: 'Oh, he's big, he needs more, you should give him solids,' because the food most people start with—pear, apple, or steamed carrot—those are things you would eat if you were going on a diet."   *Holly, mother of Ava, 7, Archie, 4, and Glen, 6 months*

♦ *True signs of readiness*

The most reliable way to tell whether your baby is ready for solid foods is to look for signs that coincide with the important changes within her body that will enable her to cope with them (that is, the development of her immune and digestive systems, and the growth and development of her mouth). If she can sit up with little or no support, reach out to grab things and take them to her mouth quickly and accurately, and if she is gnawing on her toys and making chewing movements, then the chances are she is ready to start exploring solid foods.

But the very best sign that a baby is ready is when she starts to put food into her mouth herself—which she can only do if she is given the opportunity.

> "When the child on your lap grabs a handful of your dinner from your plate, chews it, and swallows it, then it might be time to push the plate nearer to her."
>
> *Gabrielle Palmer, nutritionist and author*

Why is Some Baby Food Labeled as Suitable from Four Months?

Baby food jars and packets are often labeled "Stage 1," "Stage 2" and so on, with stage 1 foods being very smooth purées and stage 2 foods slightly lumpier. Many labels on stage 1 foods state that they are suitable for babies starting at four months old. However, most health professionals now agree that four months is too young for solids.

The result is that many parents are confused—they don't know that the official view is changing or, if they do, they don't realize why it's so important for babies under six months not to have anything other than breast milk or infant formula. So they continue to buy baby food for babies who are really too young to have it.

A voluntary code of conduct (the International Code of Marketing of Breast-milk Substitutes[5]) restricts the promotion of *any* food or drinks for babies under six months old and almost all countries of the world have signed on to it. Some (Canada and the UK, for instance) have kept it as a voluntary code while others have made it part of their law. The United States has done neither of these things, so manufacturers of baby foods and drinks in the United States are free to continue to label their products as "suitable from four months."

BLW STORY

Max has always been big for his age, 98th percentile. So I was always hearing from people about big babies, how they would be getting extra hungry, and need solids from four months, and so on. But I just let myself be guided by him.

And despite being a big baby, he didn't seem to really get into food. I could tell from his diapers that he was probably eating something from about eight months, but I don't think he was eating lots until about ten months.

I really saw the first six months of BLW as just being for him to explore tastes and textures, so I didn't worry about the fact that, compared to my friends who were feeding purées, I couldn't really tell how much he was eating. I think feeding this way took the pressure off, really. I'd tried spoon-feeding my nephews, and there was a certain amount they were supposed to eat from the jar, and I found it very stressful when they just decided to stop.

With BLW you have to be a bit relaxed about it, initially, and let them take it at their own pace. It's quite easy to just assume they're not eating anything, and that they're going to be starving, and that you need to feed them something. I used to think: "Why am I worrying? Breast milk is much more nutritious for him than half a carrot." I assumed that he was getting whatever nutrition he needed from the breast milk. And breast-feeding fit so easily around mealtimes. He just fed whenever he wanted to—and it just all came together.

Charlotte, mother of Max, 16 months

Baby-Led Weaning Isn't New

You may be reading this and thinking, "I did that—it's nothing new." If so, you're right—BLW *isn't* new, but talking about it is.

Many parents, especially those who have three or more children, have discovered almost by accident that letting the baby take the lead makes life easier and more enjoyable for everyone. Mostly, their story goes something like this: they did as they were told with their first baby, finding that weaning required a lot of patience for very little reward. They relaxed a bit with the second child, breaking some of the "rules" and discovering that weaning seemed a bit easier as a result. By the time their third baby was born they were so busy they just "let her get on with it."

The first child—spoon-fed according to all the guidelines—turned into quite a fussy eater. The second baby was a bit less picky, but the third baby became a noticeably "better" eater than the other two—less fussy and more adventurous. The parents had discovered BLW. Unfortunately, because they were worried that they would be considered bad parents—or even just plain lazy—they didn't tell anyone.

> "The more people I talk to, the more I realize that introducing solids this way is not a new idea. So many people say: 'Actually, I did that, I just didn't talk about it.' Parents have been doing this for years—it just didn't have a name."
>
> *Clare, mother of Louise, 7 months*

A Brief History of Feeding Babies

Historically, not a great deal is known about how babies were introduced to solids much before the late 19th century;

parenting skills and knowledge were passed from mother to daughter, with very little written down. But it is likely that, as today, many families discovered BLW for themselves. And although anecdotal evidence suggests that, throughout the 20th century, at least some families introduced solids this way, the story was very different for the majority of babies.

At the turn of the century, babies didn't have any solid foods until they were around eight or nine months old; by the 1960s this had dropped to as early as two or three months, and by the 1990s most babies were having solids starting around four months old. Many of these changes came about because of changes in the way babies were breast-fed; there was little sound research into infant feeding and, for a long time, no official guidelines on introducing solids.

> "My grandma thought it was great when she saw Rosy feeding herself. She was the oldest of seven children and she said that was the way she remembered her mother feeding her younger brothers and sisters. She couldn't remember any spoon-feeding at all. She said she'd only spoon-fed my mom because she was told to start at three months."
>
> Linda, mother of Rosy, 22 months

In the early 1900s, babies had only breast milk—either from their own mother or from a wet nurse (a woman employed by parents to breast-feed their baby)—for about eight or nine months, or even longer. Although smooth biscuits or hard-baked crusts would sometimes be given at around seven or eight months, these were intended only as a way of developing chewing skills or to help with teething, not as "food."

As wet-nursing became less and less popular, doctors started to see it as their role to advise mothers on how to breast-feed their own babies. Leaving things to the instinct of the mother—or even worse, her baby—was thought to be unreliable, and feeding began to be carefully controlled from the minute the baby was born.

Although breast-feeding was recognized as the best way to feed babies, the fact that they need to feed frequently for their mothers to make enough milk wasn't understood. Mothers were told to follow a strict timetable, limiting the time the baby spent at the breast and spacing feedings several hours apart. As a result, many moms "failed" to produce enough milk—and their babies "failed" to thrive. No surprise, then, that the few substitute milks available at the time began to grow in popularity and to be recommended by doctors, in an effort to make sure babies got all the nutrients they needed.

As "by the clock" feeding became more widespread and more mothers turned to the new infant formulas, it became clear to doctors that these products weren't as good for babies as their advertisements suggested. Babies fed on such formulas frequently got sick or were undernourished, and the feedings were often complicated to make up, so mistakes were common.

Since most mothers still preferred to start their babies on the breast, even if (because of the regimented feeding schedules) they were only "able" to feed them for a few months, doctors—and the authors of the newly popular parenting books—saw the answer as encouraging breast-feeding from birth but introducing "solid" foods (which were, of course, semisolid) as soon as it was clear that the mother's breast milk was no longer "enough"—usually when the baby was somewhere between two and four months of age. Chubbiness was seen as a sign of good health and mothers were urged to "fatten up" their babies, so most first foods were cereal-based.

At around the same time, preprepared sieved or "strained"

foods began appearing in stores and, by the 1930s, a variety of fruit and vegetable-based baby foods was available. These were intended for babies from about six months onward, but it was found that they could just as easily be fed to younger babies.

Once babies were routinely being given "solid" foods from well before the age they could chew, the practice of introducing teething biscuits declined. And, although the need to introduce foods that were closer to family meals was still acknowledged, babies usually progressed to lumpy foods given by spoon, rather than being given foods that they could grasp.

In the 1960s it was recognized that babies needed to practice chewing food and moving it around in their mouths if they were to become good at it, and parents were encouraged to introduce finger foods at about six months. However, because it was assumed that babies needed to get used to very soft foods *before* they could learn to chew, most people believed they had to start purées well before six months in order to be able to move on to chewable foods at the right time.

When the American Academy of Pediatrics issued its 4–6 months guidance in 1980, most babies of three months were already having something other than milk feedings (usually "baby" cereal). The guidelines said that babies shouldn't be given any solid foods until they were at least four months old and that they should all be having some other foods by the time they reached six months. This advice is only just changing, following the recommendation of the World Health Organization in 2002.

The Trouble with Spoon-Feeding

Imagine you are six months old. You enjoy copying whatever you see your family doing, and you want to grab the things they

BLW STORY

When I had my daughter I instinctively decided I wasn't going to do solids until she was ready. I'd had such a miserable experience with my first child, Jack, trying to start him on solids at four months. But that was the guidance at the time (he's now 21). Now, of course, I realize that he wasn't developmentally or psychologically up to it. He hated it.

Anna was perfectly happy just breast-feeding, so I just didn't bother with purées at all. We didn't go to the doctor's very much, but if they asked me, I just lied. I remember her eight-month checkup, and I said: "Yes, she's on three meals a day, she's loving it," when in reality, she'd only helped herself to a few pieces of food that the rest of us were eating. She went straight from breast milk to picking up food and eating it. There were no stages; no fine purée, then mash, then lumps.

This was 16 years ago—most babies would have been on three full meals by the time they were six months. People who knew I wasn't spoon-feeding her were confused, but they could see that she was fine. They probably just thought I was lazy. And when Anna did start eating, when she was a little over eight months, everyone could see she was managing normal food perfectly well, and that she was quite happy.

Lizzie, mother of Jack, 21 , Anna, 16,
and Robert, 13

are handling to find out what they are. As you watch your parents eating, you're fascinated by the smells, shapes, and colors. You don't understand that they are eating because they're hungry; you simply want to do whatever it is they're doing—that's how you learn. But instead of allowing you to join in, your parents insist on putting something mushy into your mouth with a spoon. The mush is always the same consistency but the taste seems to vary: sometimes it's nice, sometimes it's not. Your parents might let you see it, but they rarely let you touch it. At times they seem to be in a hurry; at other times you have to wait for the next mouthful. When you spit the food out because you weren't expecting it (or even just to see what it looks like) they scrape it up as quickly as they can and poke it back in again! You haven't yet learned that this mush can fill your tummy, so if you're hungry you'll probably feel frustrated because what you want is a milk feed. Maybe if you're not too hungry and the mush tastes nice, you'll go along with it—but you are still curious about what everyone else is doing and would rather be allowed to do the same.

Spoon-feeding isn't *bad*; it's simply not necessary. And, while many babies who are spoon-fed go on to enjoy mealtimes without any problems, feeding babies this way carries a *potential* for creating problems that doesn't exist with BLW. Partly this has to do with the consistency of puréed or mashed food, and partly it's to do with how much control the baby has over her eating.

- The consistency of puréed or mashed food means that it is easy to suck it off a spoon; it doesn't need to be chewed. If a baby doesn't get the chance to experiment with food that needs chewing soon after she reaches six months, the development of chewing skills can be delayed. Babies who aren't introduced to pieces of food until they are almost a year old (or later) may never learn to manage lumps well. (It's the equivalent of not giving a child the chance to walk until they're, say, three years old.) Chewing skills are important for many reasons, including the development of speech, good digestion and safe eating (see page 41).

- Babies learn to cope with lumps better and more quickly if they are allowed to feed themselves, because it's easier to manipulate and chew food when it starts off at the front of the mouth. Foods fed by a spoon tend to be sucked straight to the back of the mouth where they can't be moved around as easily—or as safely.

- Many spoon-fed babies gag on lumpy or mashed foods (sold commercially as "second stage" foods) when they are first introduced because, when they suck them off the spoon to the back of their mouth, they trigger their gag reflex (see page 46). It is more difficult for a baby to work out how to avoid gagging when she is spoon-fed than when she is putting the food into her mouth herself, and many babies simply decide to refuse the spoon.

- Being spoon-fed by someone else means the baby is not in control of how much she eats, or how quickly. Sloppy food gets swallowed quickly and it's tempting to persuade the baby to have "just one more spoonful." Often, babies eat faster than they would do otherwise and end up having more than they really need. Persistently persuading a child to eat more than she needs interferes with her ability to sense when she is full and could lead to a lifetime problem with overeating.

- Milk feedings are the most important single source of nourishment for a baby under a year old. Solids are much less nutrient-rich than either breast milk or infant formula. If a baby is given too much solid food (which can easily happen with spoon-feeding), her appetite for breast milk or formula will be reduced. As a result she may get less of some nutrients than she needs.

- Spoon-feeding is simply not as much fun for a baby as self-feeding. Babies want to explore food—that's how they learn. They don't generally like having things done *to* them or *for* them. Allowing babies to feed themselves makes mealtimes more enjoyable and encourages them to trust food—making it more likely that they will enjoy a wide range of tastes and textures.

This doesn't mean BLW babies can never have mushy foods. A few babies manage to feed themselves from a pre-loaded spoon early on, others learn to "dip" spoons fairly quickly, and there are many other ways babies can manage sloppy foods (see page 113). The problems come from giving babies *only* soft foods, and from not allowing them to have control at mealtimes.

Being in control of what she eats allows the baby to taste new foods at the front of her mouth and spit them out if she doesn't like them, whereas a spoonful of puréed food gets sucked straight to the back of the mouth and is much harder to deal with. Unless she's sure it's something she likes, the baby may refuse it. It's easy to see how this can lead to babies refusing all but the nicest tastes.

"Mealtimes became like a battleground for a couple of weeks when I was giving Mabel purées; she wouldn't even try anything off the spoon. I found it so frustrating. I don't know if it was the spoon issue, or the texture of the purée—or a combination of both. The minute I gave her something that she could feed herself and that she was in control of, mealtimes were fun for her, and she would try anything. She wouldn't touch puréed corn, but when I gave her those little baby corns, she couldn't get enough of them."

Becky, *mother of Mabel, 10 months*

In many countries everyone eats with their fingers. In fact, some cultures believe that it's important to touch and feel food to really enjoy it, and that using any sort of silverware spoils the experience; others simply don't see the need to use tools to eat with. And yet, in most Western countries, we seem convinced that you just can't get food into a baby without using a spoon.

Of course, spoon-feeding seemed to be unavoidable when it was believed that babies of three or four months needed "solids" since, at that age, they couldn't chew or get food to their mouths themselves. This led to an assumption that spoon-feeding and purées were an essential part of introducing solids, no matter what the age of the baby.

So, although research now suggests that those babies who started solids at three or four months old (or even younger) shouldn't have been having them at all, most people still assume that a baby's first solid foods should be given by spoon. There doesn't appear to be any research to back this up. Nobody seems to have investigated whether spoon-feeding is either safe or appropriate for babies—it has simply become common practice: "tried and trusted," but not actually *tested*.

> "When I was spoon-feeding Ivan I'd have to trick him into laughing to get the spoon into his mouth—but it would just come straight back out. So I'd just get it in from any angle I could before he turned his head away. He obviously didn't want it, but we were convinced he needed the food. So we would sit there, getting frustrated, watching the clock ticking while we tried to get the whole jar into him. Looking back, I can see he probably didn't need it."
>
> *Pam, mother of Ivan, 3,*
> *and Molly, 18 months*

The Benefits of BLW

It's enjoyable!

Eating should be pleasurable for everyone—adults and babies alike. Playing an active part in mealtimes and being in control of what to eat, how much to eat, and how fast to eat it make eating more enjoyable; the opposite can make mealtimes miserable. Baby-led weaning babies look forward to eating; they enjoy learning about different foods and doing things for themselves. Early experiences of happy, stress-free mealtimes are more likely to give a child a healthy attitude toward food for life.

It's natural

Babies are programmed to experiment and explore; it's how they learn. They use their hands and their mouths to find out about all sorts of objects, including food. With BLW a baby can explore food at her own pace and follow her instincts to eat when she's ready—just like any other baby animal.

Learning about food

Babies who are allowed to feed themselves learn about the look, smell, taste, and texture of different foods, and how different flavors work together; with spoon-feeding all the tastes are puréed into one. Baby-led weaning babies can discover the different tastes in, say, a chicken and vegetable casserole, and begin to learn how to recognize foods they like. And they can simply leave anything they don't like, rather than having to refuse the whole casserole to avoid it. This makes planning easier and means babies don't miss out on the foods they enjoy. It also means that the whole family can share a meal, even if not everyone likes *all* the flavors.

Learning to eat safely

Being allowed to explore food before it goes into their mouth teaches babies important lessons about what's chewable and what isn't. The relationship between what we feel with one part of our body and what we sense with another is something that can only be learned through experience. So, for a baby, feeling a piece of food in her hand and then putting it in her mouth helps her to judge how easy different sized pieces of food are to chew and to move around with her tongue. This may be an important safety feature, preventing her later from putting pieces which are too big to be chewed into her mouth. Learning from the beginning how to deal with foods with different textures may also make babies less likely to choke (see page 46).

Learning about their world

Babies never just play; they are always learning. Pretty much everything babies can learn from the best (and most expensive) educational toy can be learned by handling food. For instance, they figure out how to hold something soft without squashing it or something slippery without dropping it—and about concepts such as less and more, size, shape, weight and texture, too. Because all their senses (sight, touch, hearing, smell, and taste) are involved, they discover how to relate all these things together for a better understanding of the world around them.

Reaching potential

Feeding themselves allows babies to practice important aspects of their development at every mealtime. Using their fingers to get food to their mouths means BLW babies practice hand-eye coordination; gripping foods of different sizes and textures several times a day improves their dexterity. This may help with writing and drawing skills later. And chewing food (rather than just swallowing purées) develops the facial muscles that will be needed as they learn to talk.

> "Everyone says Emmanuel's skills with his hands are amazing for his age—but I think it's normal. Every baby should be able to do those things; it's just that they don't get the opportunity to practice the way they do if they are feeding themselves a variety of foods every day. But nobody believes me when I say it's because he's always fed himself."
>
> *Antonietta, mother of Emmanuel, 2*

Gaining confidence

Allowing babies to do things for themselves not only enables them to learn but also gives them confidence in their own abilities and judgment. When a baby picks something up and gets it to her mouth she receives an almost instant reward in the form of an interesting taste or texture. This teaches her that she is capable of making good things happen, which in turn helps to build her confidence and self-esteem. As her experience of food grows, and she discovers what's edible and what isn't and what to expect from each type of food, she learns to trust her own judgment. Confident babies grow into confident toddlers, who aren't afraid to try new things and who bounce back when things don't go their way. Seeing their

WHAT IS BABY-LED WEANING?

child feed herself helps her parents to trust her abilities and instincts. This often allows them to be more relaxed about her need to explore the world, which in turn means that the baby will have more freedom to learn.

Trusting food

Because BLW babies are allowed to use their instincts to decide what to eat and what to leave, they rarely show any suspicion of food—as is sometimes seen in other babies and toddlers. Allowing them to reject a food they feel they don't need, or that may seem unsafe (over/underripe, rancid or poisonous), means babies are more willing to try new foods because they know they'll be allowed to decide whether or not to eat them.

> "To start with, Emma was much keener on food when she could see what it was. She was a bit more cautious with anything that was mixed together, even stews. She'd still eat it, but she'd spend time examining it first, as if she needed to check it out."
>
> *Michelle, mother of Emma, 2*

Being part of family mealtimes

Baby-led-weaning babies are included in family mealtimes from the start, eating the same food and joining in the social time. This is fun for the baby and allows her to copy mealtime behavior, so that she will naturally move on to using utensils and adopt the table manners expected in her family. Babies can begin to learn about how different foods are eaten, how to share, how to wait their turn, and how to make conversation. Sharing mealtimes has a positive impact on family relationships, social skills, language development, and healthy eating.

Appetite control

Eating habits developed during childhood can last a lifetime. It seems likely that babies who are allowed to choose what to eat from a range of nutritious foods, at their own pace, and to decide when they've had enough, continue to eat according to their appetite and are less likely to overeat when they are older. This may be an important part of preventing obesity.

Better nutrition

Anecdotal evidence suggests that children whose parents adopt BLW and involve them in their meals from the beginning are less likely to choose unhealthy foods when they are older and are therefore more likely to be better nourished, long term. This is partly because they are used to copying what their parents do, and to eating adult food wherever they are, and partly because they tend to be more adventurous eaters anyway.

Long-term health

Because their milk feedings are reduced very gradually, BLW babies who are breast-fed are more likely to continue getting a good intake of breast milk for longer. Breast-feeding provides not only a perfect balance of nutrients but also protection, for both children and their mothers, against many serious illnesses.

Dealing with textures and learning to chew

Baby-led-weaning babies experience different shapes and textures of food from the very beginning, rather than all their food being the same consistency. As they have the chance to practice chewing and moving things around in their mouths, they become skilled at dealing with food more quickly than babies who are only spoon-fed. Learning to chew effectively is also good for speech and digestion (see page 41). Having the opportunity to deal with a broad range of foods from the beginning means mealtimes are more interesting for the baby and makes it more likely that she will get all the nutrients she needs.

The chance to experience real food

Baby-led weaning allows babies to experience some of the real pleasures of eating from the outset. As adults, we tend to take these for granted and forget how much the individual flavors and textures within a meal contribute to our enjoyment of it. Traditional "first-stage" baby foods often consist of several ingredients, all blended together into one smooth homogenous mixture. This not only means that the baby experiences just one texture but also that she doesn't have the chance to discover what the various ingredients taste like on their own. This has implications for her diet as well as her enjoyment of eating.

"The first time I saw a BLW baby eat I was really struck by how confident she was with ordinary, adult foods. At 10 months she was picking out pieces of food to eat, and she obviously knew what the different foods were and was used to choosing what she wanted. She seemed so content—and she was thoroughly enjoying her meal."

Maryanne, day care manager

A positive attitude toward food

Many eating disorders of childhood probably have their roots in infancy. If a baby's early experiences with food are healthy and happy, problems such as food refusal and food phobias are much less likely.

Easier, less complicated meals

Puréeing food is time-consuming and can be tedious. With BLW, it just isn't necessary. Provided the parents' diet is healthy, they can easily adapt their meals for their baby. And rather than spoon-feeding your baby separately or while your own dinner goes cold (and then having to amuse him while you eat), with BLW you and your baby get to eat together.

No mealtime battles

When there is no pressure on babies to eat, there is no opportunity for mealtimes to become a battleground. Instead, the whole family can enjoy stress-free meals together, meaning happy children and happy parents.

Less pickiness as a toddler

Pickiness and food refusal are less likely with BLW. This is because eating is enjoyable with this method and, because the baby is eating normal family foods from the start, there isn't the transition from baby foods to lumpier meals and then to family meals, which many babies find difficult.

> "I find babies who have been encouraged to have solids this way enjoy a more varied diet and seem to be less fussy with foods later on."
>
> *Beverley, public health nurse*

No need for games or tricks

Many parents who spoon-feed their baby find that she isn't keen to eat, and they have to come up with ways of persuading her to accept different foods. Because BLW respects babies' decisions about what to eat (or not to eat) and when to stop eating, the need to persuade just doesn't arise. This means there is no call for elaborate games involving train and airplane noises to try to fool a baby into accepting food she doesn't want. And there is no need to trick toddlers into eating healthily by making food into special shapes (such as smiley faces) or "hiding" vegetables in other dishes.

Eating out is easier

Baby-led weaning means that there is usually something on most restaurant menus that babies can have, especially as babies who are introduced to solids this way are likely to be adventurous eaters. Parents have the chance to enjoy their own food while it's hot. Their baby, meanwhile, is learning how a restaurant works, that her food looks and smells different from the way it is at home—and that she has to wait for it to arrive. All of this makes the experience very unlike that of a baby who is given the same food as she has at home from the same little jar. It also makes spontaneous outings much more feasible: working out what to take for the baby to eat is easy, with no concerns about preparing puréed food in advance or heating up baby food while you are out.

"I can't believe how easy it is when we go out. My granddaughter just eats what we eat. When my son was her age I always had to take jars or packets and find a way of heating it up. She tries everything we give her and has a great variety. It seems far less hassle than in my day!"

Anne, grandmother of Lilly, 9 months

It's cheaper

Letting the baby share what's being cooked for the rest of the family is cheaper than buying and preparing separate meals. And it's much less expensive than ready-made baby foods!

Are There Any Disadvantages?

The mess

Okay, yes, it *is* a bit messy! But all babies need to learn to feed themselves at some point, and that will involve some mess. It's just that, with BLW, the mess comes earlier than it would otherwise. The good news is that the messy period, for a lot of babies, is quite short; because the baby has the chance to practice feeding herself so often, she quickly gets good at it. There are lots of ways to prepare for the mess (see also page 83) and, anyway, spoon-feeding can be pretty messy, too!

Other people's worries

Dealing with the early fears and doubts of relatives and friends isn't really a disadvantage, but it can be a problem with BLW. Because it hasn't been talked about much in the

past, many people don't know about this method of introducing solids, or understand how it works. This means they
may be skeptical or worry about it—until, that is, they see it
in action.

2.

How Does Baby-Led Weaning Work?

"The beauty is that the readiness is so obvious. When a baby can sit up, reach out, pick food up and put it in his mouth, move it around and swallow it, his guts are ready. Nature would not have got it wrong."

*Hazel, mother of Evie 8 , Sam, 5,
and Jacky, 22 months*

Growing Skills

Learning to eat solid food is a natural part of a baby's development—just like crawling, walking, and talking. It's a normal part of growing up. Although some babies develop faster than others, the progress of all babies follows a set pattern, and new skills are acquired in more or less the same order for every baby. For example, most babies will learn how to do the following in this order:

- roll over
- sit up
- crawl
- stand up
- walk

This principle works for all aspects of a baby's development—including feeding.

Babies develop these skills without having to be taught them. In other words, they don't really "learn" them, they just *become able* to do them. Some skills develop gradually, and others seem to appear overnight, but they are all the result of the baby practicing movements and putting them together. These skills are developing continuously, right from the moment the baby is born. Many early movements are instinctive, but, as babies gain more control over their muscles, they begin to be able to do things purposefully.

All babies develop skills that are related to feeding themselves, although babies who have the chance to practice—by handling food—are likely to become good at them earlier than babies who are spoon-fed. Babies naturally develop feeding-related skills in this order:

- latch on to mother's breast
- reach out toward interesting things
- grab objects and take them to their mouth
- explore things with lips and tongue
- bite off a piece of food
- chew
- swallow
- pick up small objects using "pincer grip" (thumb and forefinger)

At birth, babies are able to find their own way to the breast and latch on to feed. All normal, healthy babies who are born at term have this survival skill in place. They also have a basic swallowing reflex. The suckling action used at the breast or on a bottle takes milk to the back of the baby's mouth, where the swallowing mechanism is triggered.

From about three months on, babies start finding their hands: they catch sight of them and begin to wave them in front of their face and study them. If anything touches their palm, their fist spontaneously closes around it. Gradually, they begin to bring their hands purposefully to their mouth. At this age their muscles are still not very well coordinated—babies may hit themselves in the face by mistake or seem surprised to find that they have something in their hand.

By about four months a baby can reach out toward things that interest him. As his movements become more refined, he begins to be able to move his arms and hands accurately to grab hold of interesting objects and take them to his mouth. His lips and tongue are very sensitive, and the baby uses them to learn about the taste, texture, shape, and size of everyday things.

By the time they are six months old, most babies can reach for easy-to-grab objects, pick them up in their fist, and get them to their mouth accurately. If a baby has the opportunity to look at, reach for, and grab food (rather than just toys), he will take it to his mouth. Although it looks as though he is feeding himself, he won't actually swallow the food; he'll just explore it with his lips and tongue.

Between six and nine months several abilities develop, one after the other. First, the baby manages to bite or gnaw off a small piece of food with his gums (or his teeth, if he has any). Soon after this he discovers how to keep the food in his mouth for a while and, because the size and shape of the inside of his mouth has changed and he now has more control of his tongue, he is able to move the food around and chew it. At this stage though, as long as he is sitting upright it will almost certainly fall out of his mouth rather than be swallowed.

Unlike milk (from a breast or bottle), which is sucked

BLW STORY

I'm not sure whether I would have done BLW instinctively if Arne hadn't shown me. When he was almost six months he was sitting next to my oldest child, Evie, one day as she watched TV, and he just grabbed her sandwich and took a bite out of it! But having something to eat was his choice, rather than me doing something to him; he got what he wanted when he wanted it. He was happy.

It was so different from feeding Evie. She was barely five months when we started solids, and it was horrible. I'm pretty sure I cried the first time I fed her; she couldn't sit up properly so she was in a recliner chair with purée just dribbling out of her mouth. And it was such a huge effort to express enough milk to make things runny enough.

So we'd already decided to wait a while with Arne anyway and then after he'd taken the sandwich we tried mushing some food for him but he didn't like being fed, so we thought, "Why not just give him chunks of things?"

He would eat his broccoli first and then his carrot and then he would have meat or something—he was much more balanced and self-regulated than my daughter. With her, there were definitely phases where she'd refuse a whole load of food; all the effort of puréeing and she'd not want to eat. It felt very tortuous. The whole process was just so much easier with Arne, so we are doing the same with George.

Polly, mother of Evie, 6, Arne, 4,
and George, 6 months

directly to the back of the baby's mouth, solid food needs to be actively moved there. This is something that a baby is unable to do until *after* he has discovered how to bite and chew. This means that, for a week or two at least, any food he gets into his mouth will eventually fall back out again. He will only begin to swallow it when the muscles of his tongue, cheeks and jaw are sufficiently coordinated to work together to allow this. This may well be a natural safeguard to help minimize the chances of choking. But it only works as long as it's *the baby* who puts the food into his mouth—he needs to be in control.

At around nine months the baby will develop the "pincer grip"—a way of using his thumb and forefinger to pick up small objects (or food). Before this happens it's unlikely he will be able to get anything very small (such as a raisin or a pea) to his mouth.

Babies who are allowed to feed themselves at every mealtime get lots of chances to practice these skills and quickly become confident and adept. Just as babies will walk when they are ready, so, it seems, they will start to eat solid foods when they are ready—*provided they are given the opportunity.*

Most research into babies starting solids has concentrated on *when* the baby should start and *what* the baby should be fed. The relationship between how babies develop and how they start solids has been largely overlooked. But when babies *were* observed handling food (see Appendix 1, page 221), it became clear that they instinctively know when they are ready for solid foods and that they will naturally develop the skills needed to feed themselves.

> "As soon as someone explained BLW to me, I thought, 'Of course—it makes sense!' I felt foolish for not having instinctively known it when I had my first baby. So, with

John, we knew he would feed himself; we had seen from the other two that it's perfectly possible. You don't have to do finger foods as an extra to spoon-feeding, it can be the only way of feeding."

Liz, mother of Heather, 8, Edwin, 5,
and John, 20 months

Baby-Led Weaning and Breast-feeding

Self-feeding is natural for babies, whether they are breast-fed or bottle-fed. All babies are curious about their surroundings and, from around five months of age, they're beginning to pick things up and take them to their mouths. However, breast-feeding plays a specific role in preparing babies for solid foods. Here's how it works:

- *Breast-feeding babies feed themselves at the breast.* The mother has to hold her baby in a suitable position but the baby does the feeding, by scooping the breast into his mouth, then letting it go when he's had enough. In fact, it's impossible to force a baby to breast-feed—as you'll know if you've tried it. So breast-fed babies are used to feeding themselves long before they start solids. A baby who is bottle-fed relies more on his mother to take the lead. He waits for her to put the nipple into his mouth and expects her to keep it there for as long as he needs.

- *Breast-fed babies are always in control.* They can vary how fast they feed and how much milk they take according to how hungry or thirsty they are. In contrast, the pace of a bottle-fed baby's feeding is mainly determined by the size of the hole in the nipple. And it's possible to persuade him to take more milk than he really wants, simply by wiggling the nipple in his mouth to make him suck (the sucking reflex is an unavoidable response—like a knee-jerk reflex).

- *Breast-feeding uses the muscles of the mouth in a different way from bottle-feeding.* The action of the baby's mouth during breast-feeding is similar to chewing, whereas bottle-feeding is closer to sucking through a straw. So the muscles of a bottle-fed baby's mouth aren't being prepared for chewing in the same way. This may mean that he takes slightly longer to learn to move food around his mouth effectively.

- *The flavor of breast milk varies from feeding to feeding, according to what the mother has eaten.* So the breast-fed baby is used to a variety of tastes from the very beginning, whereas the baby who is formula-fed experiences only one taste. This means that the breast-fed baby will be less surprised by foods with different flavors, so will probably be more eager to experiment. By contrast, parents of formula-fed babies sometimes find that their baby is reluctant to try too many new flavors at once.

However, just because BLW is such a natural transition for breast-fed babies doesn't mean it will be difficult for the formula-fed baby—it may simply take him a little longer to get going and be as adventurous as a breast-fed baby. Some other aspects of BLW will be slightly different for the formula-fed baby, too; for example, how drinks are introduced (see page 101) and how to reduce his formula intake as his intake of solid food increases (see page 129), but the overall concept can work extremely well for all babies.

"Many mothers who have exclusively breast-fed for six months seem to find BLW the preferred option when starting their babies on solid food, and they can go on breast-feeding, too, with all of those health advantages."

Nicky, breast-feeding adviser

INTERRUPTING SELF-FEEDING

Babies are able to feed themselves (from their mother's breast) at birth and most parents wouldn't expect to have to feed a child of two or three years old—they would expect him to feed himself. It doesn't seem logical that the natural progression of self-feeding should be interrupted at six months, by introducing spoon-feeding, only for parents then to have to decide when to allow the baby to go back to feeding himself.

From six months babies can feed themselves solid food; there is no need to step in and do things for them for a few months—and no need to decide when to step out again. The baby can just carry on feeding himself all the way through.

The Motivation to Feed

The motivation for a six-month-old baby to take food to his mouth has nothing to do with hunger. Babies want to copy what others do, partly because they are curious and partly because their instinct tells them that this is the way to be sure that what they do is safe. So we shouldn't be surprised that they want to handle the food they see their parents picking up.

Most of our development as babies—maybe even all of it—is connected to survival. A baby needs to know which foods are safe and which are poisonous, so he watches his parents closely to see what they put in their mouths. This starts to happen at around the same time as he begins to work out how to use his arms and hands to grab things.

A baby's curiosity is so intense that if he wants to grab an object he will keep practicing the movements needed to get it, over and over again. And when he does manage to pick up something new, he almost always takes it to his mouth for exploring and testing. So when a baby first puts *food* in his mouth he is treating it just as he would a toy or any other object. Until he gets it there he has no idea that it has a taste, or that it is edible. If he manages to bite a piece off, he will munch it with his gums, discovering what it feels and tastes like. He is very unlikely to swallow it, partly because he doesn't want to, but mostly because he can't. He is not yet able to move a piece of food to the back of his mouth on purpose and, provided he is sitting upright and is not distracted, it is not likely to get there by accident. It will probably fall out of his mouth instead.

A baby who is allowed to take food to his mouth as soon as he can learns about the different textures and tastes of food long before he is able to swallow any. And he only very gradually discovers that food can make him feel full. His motivation for handling food only changes once he has made the connection with hunger. This is usually any time from eight months to a year or so. This timing is perfect, since it's not until then that he really begins to need the food to provide him with nutrients.

Key points

- A baby's motivation to put food in his mouth is curiosity and copying—not hunger.
- For the first couple of months or so, solid food is all about learning.

Needing Extra Nutrients

There is a myth that breast milk changes at around six months and is no longer "enough" for a baby. In fact, the breast milk produced by the mother of a six-month-old baby—or even a two-year-old—has almost exactly the same nutritional value as it has always had; what changes is the baby's need for certain nutrients. Breast milk continues to be the single most nutritiously balanced food for babies and children almost indefinitely.

Babies are born with stores of nutrients accumulated during their time in the womb. These stores start to be used from the moment the baby is born but the amounts in his milk feedings are enough to ensure that he still has plenty. From six months onward, the balance shifts, so that the baby begins *very gradually* to need more from his diet than breast milk or formula alone can supply.

It's important to recognize that, at six months, most babies are only just *beginning* to outgrow their milk-only diet. Most full-term babies have adequate stores of, for example, iron, to see them through for quite a bit longer without a problem—they don't run out of anything overnight. But they need to be introduced to solids at around six months so that they can develop the skills they need to eat different foods and get used to new tastes, ready for when they really do begin to rely on other foods as their main source of nourishment.

A baby's slowly increasing need for more nutrients seems to coincide with the gradual development of his self-feeding skills. So at six months, when they still have a good store of nutrients, almost all babies are beginning to be able to pick food up and take it to their mouths. By around nine months, when the need for more nutrients is growing, most BLW babies have developed the skills they need to eat a wide range of family foods, which will provide them with the extra nourishment they need. It's at about this age (though it varies quite a bit from baby to baby) that many BLW parents report their baby seems to be eating more purposefully—as though he instinctively knows that he actually *needs* this food in addition to his milk or formula.

Moving Away from Milk Feedings

Many parents feel under pressure to reduce their child's milk feedings so that he relies more on solid foods, but this shouldn't be rushed. Between six and nine months, the amount of breast milk or formula should stay more or less the same while solid foods gradually increase. It's only from about nine months that milk feedings begin to be reduced and solids start to take over. If a baby is allowed to determine the start of solid feeding and the pace of its progress he will follow his own natural path toward more solids and less milk.

Babies vary enormously in the pace at which they come to grips with solid feeding and then begin to move away from breast milk or formula. Some babies start swallowing food almost straight away (at six months), and by nine months they are competent self-feeders who are already beginning to cut down their milk feedings.

Other babies start very gradually, showing no real interest

in doing more than exploring solid foods until they are well over eight months, and still eating only small amounts at 10 or even 12 months.

And of course, there are many variations in between. There are babies who start off very enthusiastically but who seem to slow down after a few weeks. And there are those who seem to take ages to take any interest in solids—but, once they do, develop with amazing speed.

Many babies do things in bursts, alternating weeks when nothing much seems to happen with weeks when they're doing something new every day. All of this is completely normal—and is very different from the sort of steady, stage-by-stage progress that parents are led to expect when their baby is on puréed foods.

> "One of the problems I have with conventional weaning is the 'stages' babies are supposed to go through; BLW blows all that out of the water."
>
> *Helen, dietitian*

Developing the Ability to Chew

The way a baby is able to use his mouth matures alongside his other abilities. Chewing, swallowing, and speech all rely on coordinated movements of the muscles of the mouth, including the tongue. Young babies can coordinate these muscles to enable breast-feeding (or bottle-feeding) but that's all. That's why if "solid" food is given to very young babies it has to be very soft and runny, because the only way the baby can manage it is by sucking.

Many people assume that babies need to be spoon-fed before they can cope with foods that are truly "solid"—but this isn't the case. Babies naturally become able to manage chewable foods as their mouths grow and develop. From the beginning breast-feeding, in particular, develops muscles that will be used later for chewing and speaking.

In the past it was believed that babies had to get used to a spoon before they could move on to lumpy foods; this is not true, either. Young babies have a reflex called the "tongue thrust," which they use (unconsciously) to push anything but the breast or bottle out of their mouth. This is probably a safety mechanism, to prevent anything solid from being swallowed or inhaled. Early spoon-feeding involves trying to override the tongue thrust, which is why it's so difficult and messy. The tongue thrust reflex naturally begins to fade from about four months of age, whether or not the baby has been spoon-fed. So what was, for many years, assumed to be evidence of a baby "getting used to the spoon" was in fact just the tongue thrust reflex disappearing.

In the same way, babies don't *learn* to chew, they just develop the ability to do it, so there is no need for them to be "taught" to chew by starting them off on smooth purées and progressing gradually through mashed to lumpy food.

As adults, we tend to take for granted the way we use the muscles of our mouth. But the way you move chewing gum from one cheek to the other, how you remove the pit from a cherry or an olive and spit it out, or what you do to retrieve a fish bone or a piece of food that is stuck in your teeth are quite complex movements. Learning to move food around your mouth is important for safety as well as for eating and speaking—and the best way to learn these skills is to practice them on lots of foods with different textures.

Different textures also add to the pleasure and interest of eating; it's not just taste that makes food enjoyable. Imagine how boring it would be for adults if all our food was the same

BABIES DON'T NEED TEETH TO CHEW

Babies of six months quite often have one or more teeth, but not all do. Whether or not their teeth have started to come through doesn't seem to make much difference in their ability to bite or gnaw foods—they simply use their gums. It certainly makes no difference in whether or not they can chew. (However, they'll probably have to wait until they have more teeth to be able to bite into hard foods, such as a raw carrot.) Gums are very good for biting and munching—as any breast-feeding mother who has had a nip from a teething baby will tell you!

> "Otis hasn't got any teeth yet. The other two didn't get any teeth at all until they were over a year old so I know babies don't need teeth to chew—at a year they were both eating normal family foods."
>
> *Sadie, mother of Ellen, 9, Thomas, 5,*
> *and Otis, 8 months*

texture (especially if it was all mashed or puréed). Crunchy, chewy, sticky, and runny foods all produce different sensations in the mouth and need to be managed in a different way. The more a baby is allowed to experience different textures the more likely he is to become skilled at dealing with them and the more willing he'll be to try new foods.

The "Window of Opportunity"

Some people refer to the period between four and six months as a "window of opportunity" for getting babies used to new tastes and textures. They worry that, if this "window" is missed, the baby will be reluctant to accept solid foods and weaning will be difficult as a result. This concern seems to stem from the fact that babies who don't have their first spoonful of solid food until after they reach six months appear to be more resistant to the idea than younger babies.

Unfortunately, because spoon-feeding has become the accepted way to feed babies, nobody has really questioned whether it might be the *feeding* that these babies are refusing, rather than the *food*. Babies of six months and older who are allowed to self-feed are in fact very keen to try new foods; they are also capable little people who like to do things for themselves. So if there *is* an ideal period for babies to get used to new tastes and textures, it doesn't start until they naturally begin to take food to their mouths, at around six months.

Eating Enough but Not Too Much: Learning Appetite Control

Knowing when to stop eating is a key factor in avoiding obesity and maintaining the right weight for your size, however old you are, so stopping when you are full sounds like common sense. But many children—and adults—are unable to do this.

Many parents worry that their baby or child isn't eating enough. Food is intrinsically linked with nurturing and love: we all want to show our babies how much we love them and feeding them is one way to do this. At the same time, we can feel a sense of rejection when our child turns down the food we have prepared for him. These emotions, combined with unrealistic expectations of how much food babies should eat (see page 142), mean that many babies—and older children—are regularly persuaded to eat more than they need. This can mean that the child simply learns to overeat or, in extreme cases, it can lead to problems such as food refusal or phobias; either way, the development of normal appetite control is at risk.

Persuading young babies to eat food they don't want is especially easy to do if they are spoon-fed. Babies who are allowed to feed themselves will naturally manage their own intake— they simply stop eating when they are full. This means they eat as much as they need—and no more.

How fast we eat is also important. If a baby is allowed to feed himself he will eat at his own pace, taking as much time as he needs to deal with a particular piece of food. Parents are often surprised at how long their baby can spend chewing one mouthful. Being in control of how much and how quickly he eats not only makes the meal more enjoyable for him, but means that the baby is able to recognize more easily when he is full. Spoon-feeding, on the other hand, can encourage babies to eat more quickly than they would do naturally, interfering with the sensation that tells them when they have had enough. Eating too fast is another aspect of food behavior that has been linked with obesity in adults and children.

"Erin has a great attitude to food. She can control her own appetite—she simply eats when she's hungry and stops when she's full. Our eating is so messed up in this country it's really hard for some people to understand how good that is." *Judith, mother of Erin, 2*

"I found with spoon-feeding it was harder to know whether or not Tristan had actually finished when he didn't want any more—or whether it was part of the power game as to who was going to have the spoon." *Andrew, father of Tristan, 4, and Madeleine, 7 months*

Won't He Choke?

Many parents (and grandparents and others) are worried that babies who feed themselves will choke, but, provided the baby is in control of any food that goes into his mouth and he is sitting upright, BLW doesn't make choking any more likely than spoon-feeding—and may even make it less likely.

Often worries about choking are based on seeing babies *gagging* on food and confusing this with choking; these two mechanisms are related, but they are not the same thing. Gagging is a retching movement that pushes food away from the airway if it is too big to be swallowed. The baby opens his mouth and pushes his tongue forward; sometimes a piece of food appears at the front of his mouth and he may even vomit a little. It's usually over very quickly and doesn't seem to bother babies who are feeding themselves—they mostly carry on eating as if nothing had happened.

In an adult, the gag response is triggered near the back of the tongue—you have to put your finger right back toward your throat to make it happen. However, this reflex is triggered much farther forward on the tongue of a six-month-old baby, so not only is it activated more easily in a baby than it is in an adult, it also operates when the piece of food that has caused it is much farther away from the airway. So when babies of six or seven months gag on food it doesn't mean the food is too close to their airway and it very rarely means they are in danger of choking.

The gag reflex may well be a key part of babies' learning how to manage food safely. When a baby has triggered this reflex a few times, by putting too much food into his mouth or pushing it too far back, he learns not to do it. As he gets older, *whether or not he has been allowed to experiment with self-feeding*, the place where this reflex is triggered moves back along his tongue, so that gagging doesn't happen until food is nearer the back of his mouth. So he simply "outgrows" the tendency to gag.

However, as the gag reflex moves back toward its adult position it becomes less and less effective as an early-warning sign. So babies who haven't been allowed to explore food from the beginning may miss the opportunity to use it to help them learn how to keep food away from their airway. Anecdotal evidence suggests that babies who have been spoon-fed have more problems with gagging and "choking" when they start to handle food (often at around eight months) than those who have been allowed to experiment much earlier.

However, while gagging is not a cause for concern, it's important to remember that this response is essentially a safety mechanism. For it to work effectively the baby must be sitting upright, so that any food that has gone too far back in his mouth is pushed forward—not backward—by the reflex.

GAGGING, CHOKING, AND SPOON-FEEDING

Many instances of babies gagging or "choking" are actually related to spoon-feeding, especially when lumpy foods are given by spoon. To understand why this is, think about how you use a spoon to eat tomato soup and compare it with the way you eat your breakfast cereal. If you were to "slurp" your cereal the way you do your soup, the lumps would go straight to the back of your throat and you would soon start to cough and splutter. When babies are spoon-fed they tend to suck the food in, so they gag or "choke" very easily.

Choking happens when the airway is either completely or partially blocked. When something partially blocks a baby's airway, he automatically starts to cough to clear it; this is usually very effective. If the blockage is total, which is very rare, the baby is unable to cough and needs someone else to dislodge the lump for him (using standard first-aid measures).

The coughing and spluttering that look and sound so alarming are actually signs that the baby is dealing with the problem. Normal babies have a very efficient coughing reflex and, provided they are upright or leaning forward, it is usually best not to disturb them while they are clearing their airway.

"To start with, when Izaak coughed when he was eating, we would jump up, get him out of the chair and hit him on the back. But when we stopped and actually looked at what he was doing we realized that if we just allowed him the time to cough something back up, it would always come out and he would just carry on eating quite happily." *Lucy, mother of Izaak, 8 months*

Two factors make choking more likely:

- someone else putting the food (or drink) into the baby's mouth
- a leaning-back position

If someone approached you with a bowl and spoon and started to spoon-feed you the chances are you would reach out to stop them so that you could check what the food was and how much was on the spoon. You would want to control when and how it went into your mouth. These basic checks would let you predict how to deal with the food once it was in your mouth; planning how to deal with food helps to prevent choking.

If you were leaning back, being fed by someone else would be even more frightening because gravity would be more likely to take the food to the back of your mouth before you were ready to swallow it. When we relate this to adults it's clear that the person who is eating instinctively needs to, and *should*, be in control of the feeding process. The same thing applies to babies.

When a baby puts a piece of food into his mouth himself, he is *in control of it*. If he is able to chew it, he will. If he is able to get it to the back of his throat, he'll swallow it. If he isn't able to do these things then, as long as he is upright, the food will simply fall out. Allowing a baby to feed himself means that he is in control—and having control helps to keep him safe.

The link between what the baby can do with his hands and what he can do with his mouth may also help to keep the BLW baby safe. When a six-month-old baby first starts to feed himself he can't pick up the sorts of food that he might have trouble moving around with his tongue, such as raisins and peas, so they are unlikely to get into his mouth. It's only as he gets older (about nine months) that he will begin to use his finger and thumb in the "pincer grip" that enables him to pick up tiny objects. By this time, provided he has been allowed to practice feeding himself with foods of different textures, his chewing skills will be well advanced. This means that once he *can* get a raisin to his mouth he will almost certainly be able to manage it safely. This coming-together of two key aspects of babies' development is a fundamental part of what makes BLW a safe approach.

So, provided the baby is supported (if necessary) in an upright position, is in control of what goes into his mouth, and is not given foods that are an obvious choking hazard (see page 96), there is no reason to be more concerned about choking with BLW than with any other method of introducing solids.

"Magnus (who was spoon-fed) sometimes puts too much food in his mouth and then gags—and sometimes almost chokes. This happens often with meat (my husband had to pull some squid out of his mouth once, and I've had to whack him on the back hard once or twice). Leon (who was BLW'd) gagged a few times, but he has never choked."

Joy, mother of Magnus, 6, and Leon, 3

Do Babies Really Know What They Need to Eat?

Baby-led weaning babies are allowed to choose what they want (or need) to eat from the foods offered at mealtimes, and their parents are often surprised by how well balanced the baby's chosen diet is over the course of a week or so. There has been little reliable research into whether babies really *do* know what to eat instinctively, but an extraordinary experiment in the 1920s and 1930s by an American pediatrician, Dr. Clara Davis,[1] is certainly food for thought.

At the time of the research, many children were refusing to eat the foods that were considered good for them. Most pediatricians gave parents strict instructions about what, how much, and how often their child was to be fed. But Dr. Davis suspected that it was this very strictness that was the cause of the problem and that telling—or even forcing—children to eat certain foods made things worse. She had a theory that babies knew best when it came to what they needed to eat.

She devised a "self-selection" diet for infants and young children to see what would happen if babies were allowed to choose what to eat for themselves. She studied 15 children for anywhere between six months and four and a half years; all the children were between seven and nine months old when the experiment started and had been exclusively breast-fed up until that point.

The babies were offered 33 foods in all, with a slightly different selection laid out at each meal. All the foods were presented separately, mashed and unseasoned; combined foods such as bread and soup weren't allowed.

The babies could choose whatever they wanted from these foods, in any quantity. They either fed themselves or pointed to a dish and were spoon-fed by a nurse, who was not allowed to influence their decisions. If a child ate the whole portion of a particular food, more of the same food was provided—until he or she eventually stopped eating.

Meals were scrutinized in detail, so that the researchers could work out exactly what each child had eaten. Blood and urine tests and X-rays were taken to monitor the children's health.

At the end of the experiment Dr. Davis discovered that each child had chosen an extremely well-balanced diet. They were all well nourished and healthy—even those who hadn't been at the start—and they all ate a greater variety and quantity of food than was considered normal for their age. Their weight gain was above average, and they were largely free from many of the deficiency diseases (such as rickets) and other illnesses that were common at the time.

However, each child's combination of foods was unique and unpredictable—there wasn't anything approaching an "average" diet. For example, some chose to eat lots of fruit while others seemed to prefer meat; food crazes or bingeing were common (one toddler apparently ate seven eggs in one day!) All the children were also willing to try unfamiliar foods. None of them chose the cereal and milk-based diet that babies were "supposed" to eat at the time.

According to Dr. Davis, part of the reason the children were all so well nourished was that only nutritious, unprocessed foods were provided—there were no rich, fatty, or sugary foods. But simply providing a selection of good foods didn't guarantee a balanced diet. Any of the children studied could still have decided to limit their diet—by avoiding meat, or fruit and vegetables, for example—and become ill as a result. But they all ate enough of each type of food to ensure the right balance.

However, the results of the experiment aren't reliable enough to prove that Dr. Davis's theory is true. (It was a small study, and most of the data were lost—and it will never be repeated because her methods would be considered unethical today.) But the experiment became widely known at the time—it was even included in some editions of Dr. Benjamin Spock's best-selling parenting books in the 1940s and 1950s—and gradually the limited infant diet that had been so common went out of fashion. Although the message about the importance of giving babies a range of foods has persisted, the idea that they might be allowed to choose seems to have been lost—probably because in later years babies began to be given solids at three or four months, when they aren't capable of choosing what to eat.

Q&A

Will my baby be well nourished using this method?

Whether or not your baby is well nourished is up to you and your baby. Whichever approach you use, it's your responsibility to offer foods that are nutritious and that will provide a balanced diet for your baby—the difference with BLW is that what he actually eats is up to him.

BLW STORY

Our second child, Saskia, would sit on my lap while we ate and she started reaching for food from our plates when she was almost six months. She was happy grabbing food and putting it in her mouth, so we sort of intuitively did BLW without really thinking about it. And later I realized there were other people who were doing it and it had a name. It is so easy; mothers must have been doing it, especially with second babies, for generations.

In retrospect, I think our first child, Lily, was reaching for food, but we just did what is accepted wisdom for feeding babies—we spoon-fed her. We'd take turns; one of us would eat, and the other would feed Lily.

Baby-led weaning is quicker and easier—and messier. It *is* messy. But spoon-feeding is complicated. It's another little thing to be slightly anxious about. And it's boring—we were always either preparing food, or feeding, or cleaning up. It was so food-oriented, the purée thing. This seems to be much more just enjoying mealtimes and playing. It's much more relaxed.

Suzanne, mother of Lily, 3,
and Saskia, 14 months

There is a myth that babies whose eating is controlled by their parents will eat the right foods, whereas those who are allowed to choose will live on chips and chocolate. In fact, the opposite is probably true. Many parents who spoon-feed their children report that they have terrible trouble getting them to eat good food, often having to resort to tricks, such as "hiding" vegetables in other foods or feeding them in front of the TV (so they don't notice what they are eating), or promising treats if they eat their greens. By contrast, most parents who have tried BLW say their child eats a huge variety of foods without needing to be persuaded, including those that children are supposed to dislike, such as cabbage.

There is some evidence that children will naturally choose good foods, in the right quantities, if they are given the opportunity (as we've just noted, with regard to the work of Dr. Clara Davis). This needs further research, but the idea is supported by the fact that many of the stories about picky eaters come from families where the introduction of solids was controlled by the parents. Almost all of those who have tried both methods say that they wouldn't go back to the conventional approach because their BLW baby eats so much better than their other child.

> "William didn't have any purées at all, and it was quite a success. He's not a fussy eater like his brother, Samuel, who was spoon-fed. He loves the kind of things that most children won't touch; he likes black pepper and spicy food. People have said the range of food that William eats is quite amazing, compared to other children. He'll try anything."
>
> *Pete, father of Samuel, 5, William, 2, and Edward, 6 months*

Isn't puréed food easier to digest and therefore more nourishing?

It is probably true that food arriving in the stomach in puréed form is easier to digest than food in large pieces. But mouths were designed to mash food—or "purée" it—by chewing. Food that is thoroughly chewed is easier for the stomach to deal with than food that has been puréed by a blender because mixing saliva with food helps to kick-start the digestive process—especially the digestion of starchy foods.

Babies who are allowed to eat at their own pace tend to keep food in their mouths for a long time before they swallow it. During this time it is being softened with saliva and mashed by the gums. But puréed foods hardly meet with saliva at all. Instead they are sucked off the spoon straight to the back of the throat and immediately swallowed—without any chewing.

Puréeing food—especially fruit and vegetables—can also destroy some of its nutrients. When food is cut up, some of the vitamin C is lost from the exposed surfaces. Puréeing increases this loss, so food that is puréed in advance will be lower in vitamin C than it would have been if it had been eaten in large pieces. A whole apple, for example, will provide more vitamin C than the same apple puréed or mashed. Vitamin C is an important vitamin, especially as it encourages the absorption of iron. The body isn't able to store vitamin C, so it's important to have a good source every day.

It's easy to assume that puréed food is more easily digested because of what appears in the baby's diapers. Unlike the stool of a baby fed on purées, the stool of a baby eating "real" food occasionally contains pieces of vegetable, for example, in small, recognizable lumps. This doesn't mean none of the food has been digested—it just shows that the baby is learning to chew and that his body is adapting to solids. Puréed food just *looks* as though it has been more fully digested because it doesn't stand out in the diaper.

Babies who are fed too quickly (which can easily happen with spoon-feeding) may miss out on learning to chew thoroughly. Babies who have been allowed to feed themselves from the beginning and who haven't been rushed while they are eating generally take smaller mouthfuls and spend longer chewing before they swallow. This leads to better overall digestion.

Puréed foods are, of course, good for people who have difficulty chewing, but normal, healthy babies don't need to have their food puréed for them any more than normal, healthy adults do.

My doctor said that my infant should start eating some solid food once his birth weight doubles. What if that happens before he is six months old?

Weight used to be used as a guide to a baby's readiness for solid foods, but that was before we knew what we do now about babies' digestive systems. In those days infant feeding was pretty much guesswork and a key aim was for a baby to gain as much weight as possible, as quickly as possible. Having a big baby was the sign of a "good mother," and the reward was being allowed to start your baby on solids—so doubling the birth weight was something to aim for.

We now know that the readiness of the gut to digest solid foods effectively and safely is dependent on a baby's maturity, not his size. A baby who grows fast in the early months may double his birth weight in as little as four months, but that doesn't mean he is ready for solids. At the same time, the fact that a baby has still not doubled his birth weight by the time he reaches six months is not a reason to stop him from exploring solid foods. His general development (such as his ability to sit and reach out) is a much better guide to his readiness for solids than his weight.

Are there any babies who shouldn't be introduced to solid foods this way?

Baby-led weaning relies on the development of normal abilities in the baby, so it may not be suitable for absolutely all babies. Babies who have delayed development, muscle weakness or physical deformities of the mouth, hands, arms or back (such as Down syndrome, cerebral palsy, or spina bifida) may do better with spoon-feeding, or with a combination of spoon-feeding and finger foods. However, finger foods shouldn't be ruled out for these babies, since they can sometimes be an ideal way to help them develop precisely those skills that they find difficult. Some babies with digestive disorders may need special foods that can't be made into suitable shapes for self-feeding, but this shouldn't prevent them from having their other foods this way.

Premature babies may also have different needs when it comes to introducing solids, but it really depends on how many weeks premature the baby was. While a pregnancy of 36 or 37 weeks can be considered almost full-term, one of only 27 weeks clearly cannot. Also, many premature babies are not just born early but are also extremely small, or even ill, or there may be reasons why they were born early that have a bearing on their later development. Clearly, one recommendation won't do for them all.

Baby-led weaning works for a baby born at term, because his nutritional need for solid food and his developmental readiness—or ability—to feed himself coincide, so he can feed himself with solids as soon as he needs to (usually sometime soon after six months). A premature baby's general development continues at more or less the same pace as if he had been born when he was due—so if he is six weeks early he probably won't show an interest in food or be able to get it to his mouth until he is around seven and a half months. But it's quite possible that he will need some additional nutrients before this because he hasn't had enough time in the womb to build up the normal reserves.

Not a great deal is known about the needs of preterm babies when it comes to solid food. In particular, it's not clear whether, for those babies who need them before they are able to feed themselves, additional nutrients are best given as puréed food (in which case a short period of spoon-feeding will be necessary) or as prescribed supplements in the form of medicine. Each baby needs to be treated as an individual. However, there is no reason why babies who don't need additional nutrients (or who are having them as medicine) shouldn't be allowed to take their time with solids, even if this means they don't start showing an interest until they are well past six months.

In general, all babies of six months or more can be encouraged to explore food with their hands and to experiment with feeding themselves as soon as they appear interested. However, if your baby was born prematurely or has particular medical or physical problems, you should seek advice from your baby's pediatrician, pediatric dietitian, and/or speech and language therapist before deciding whether to use BLW as the only method for introducing your baby to solid foods.

> "Sean was born four weeks early and, when I started BLW, it all felt quite new to me, having spoon-fed Lorna. I think he was a little 'behind' his peers as they were all term babies, but doing BLW gave him the chance to show us when he was ready."
>
> Rachel, mother of Lorna, 14, and Sean, 4

My baby just seems so much hungrier now that he is four months old. Will it hurt if I feed him a bit of rice cereal and then move on to BLW?

Most babies really don't need anything other than milk feedings until they are at least six months old but, in recent decades, some of the things that babies do at around four months have been seen as signs of readiness for solids (see page 6). For example, many babies at this age start to watch keenly when their parents are eating, but this is just part of their natural curiosity about everything their parents do—it isn't a sign of hunger.

Some four-month-old babies begin to be more wakeful at night; this may have nothing to do with hunger or it may be a sign that the baby is having a "growth spurt" (also known as an "appetite spurt"). If your baby does need extra food at this age, then increasing his milk feedings is all that's necessary. Giving him more milk, rather than solids, is the best way to ensure that the balance of his nutrition remains good.

Rice cereal used to be recommended as the first "solid" food for babies, but we now know that rice isn't easy for babies under six months to digest. It's also low in key nutrients (even when cereals are "fortified" with minerals and vitamins, babies may not be able to absorb these easily). Giving rice can also mean that babies take less breast milk or formula, so their overall nutrition is *reduced*, not improved. Even at six months, rice cereal is not the best food for babies to start with.

If you have already started your baby on cereal, see page 92 for the best way to progress to BLW, and page 200 for information on spoon-feeding alongside baby-led weaning.

Is it really appropriate to let the baby take control?

Learning to eat solid foods is a natural stage of development. We don't control when a baby starts to walk, so it's not clear why we should control his move to solid foods. No parent would actively prevent their baby from walking when he is showing signs of doing it—it would be seen as cruel and potentially harmful. But many parents, without realizing it, exert *negative* control over their baby's instinct to eat, by preventing him from feeding himself or not allowing him to make any decisions at mealtimes.

As a parent, the only control you need to have over your baby's feeding is deciding which foods he is offered, and how often. Provided you offer him nutritious food, it should be your baby's decision what he eats, how much, and how fast.

The best way to ensure that a breast-fed baby gets the right amount of milk (and to minimize health problems for his mother) is to allow him to control the feeding from the very beginning—how often he feeds, how fast, and for how long. This is known as demand feeding or baby-led feeding. Taking a baby-led approach to the introduction of solids simply allows your baby to use the same sort of control during the transition to family meals. This means he can continue to respond to his internal cues of feeling either hungry or full and eat as much or as little as he needs. This is the basis for natural appetite control and a healthy attitude toward food throughout life.

If a baby is bottle-fed, milk feedings tend to be controlled by his parents in terms of timing and amount. But this control will have to be relinquished at some time. So when is the right time? Why not when the baby starts solid foods? This would seem to be the ideal opportunity to allow a baby to develop his natural instinct for eating according to his needs.

Many parents prefer to spoon-feed babies and young children simply because it is quicker than allowing them to feed themselves.

But, as adults, it's important for us to be able to decide how long we take over a meal. Sometimes we want to relax and really enjoy the food; other times we need to just eat and run. Nobody would want that decision to be made by someone else—especially if they were spoon-feeding us! Rushing our food means we don't enjoy it as much, and it may interfere with digestion. Allowing a baby to pace himself will help him to enjoy his food more—and possibly reduce the risk of tummy ache and constipation.

Controlling how babies eat doesn't lead to better nutrition or better behavior—in fact, it's more likely to lead to mealtime battles. Babies seem to have an instinct to test new foods slowly, in their own time. Evidence from work on children's eating disorders suggests that not allowing them to do this may make them fearful of new foods, while controlling or manipulating babies in other ways, such as tricking them (for instance, by alternating spoonfuls of sweet food and savory food), teaches them not to trust the feeding process.

It's easy to see, too, that rushing children when they eat can lead to them eating too fast and not chewing thoroughly—and perhaps not eating all they need. Coaxing, on the other hand, teaches them to eat *more* than they need. In extreme cases, this kind of manipulation can put children off food altogether.

Many of the eating problems that affect older children and their families have their roots in issues of control. Indeed, health professionals who work with these families commonly start by asking the parents to "give control back to the child." Maybe if this control isn't taken away in the first place, problems like these won't be as common.

> "I like the fact that, with BLW, the baby is in control. I see lots of babies who are dysfunctional feeders, and it's nearly always because they have no control."
>
> *Helen, dietitian*

3.

Getting Started

"Lara sat at the table with us while we ate for a few weeks before she had her first taste of food. She would follow the food to our mouths with her eyes and 'air chew' along with us. Then one day she took some bread from my hand, stared at it for a while, and slowly brought it to her mouth. She missed and poked herself in the cheek. I had to fight the urge to help her, and eventually she found her mouth. She sucked and chomped on the bread—I don't think she actually swallowed anything. But the excitement and pride I felt was ridiculous."

Emma, mother of Lara, 7 months

Preparing for BLW

Once your baby is approaching six months, you may find that she wants to join in with family mealtimes, even though she is not quite ready to start solids. Babies are intensely curious at this age and are happiest when they feel included. Letting your baby sit with you and giving her a cup or spoon to play with will make her feel part of what's going on. When she's ready to move on to handling food, she'll let you know.

You don't have to buy any special equipment for BLW, and although there are some products that may make your life a little easier, they aren't essential. A high chair may be useful, but many parents start offering solids simply by sitting their baby on their lap during mealtimes and letting her play with food from their plate. Whatever you decide, once your baby begins exploring food, make sure she is safe (i.e., she can't fall), and that she is supported in a fully upright (vertical) position. (Leaning back while eating can be dangerous, so never let your baby eat in a reclining bouncy chair or a car seat.)

Normal, healthy family foods can be adapted easily so that your baby can manage them, so there's no need to buy or prepare any special foods for her (see Chapter 4 for more on what to offer and the few foods you need to avoid). And there's no need for any silverware for the first few months, as your baby will use her fingers; just make sure her hands are clean before she starts.

Finally, you may want to prepare for some mess—a baby learning about food can be very messy in the early months (see page 84 for tips).

> "James always sat on my lap at mealtimes, and he started grabbing food and getting it to his mouth at about seven months. One of the first things he had was a really tender piece of steak! I made a stew and I offered him a big chunk of meat and he just sucked on it and maybe gummed some of the fibers. He looked as if he was really enjoying it." *Sarah, mother of James, 2*

When to "Eat"

Although many books on introducing solids suggest timetables for feeding babies in the first few weeks or months, this isn't necessary with BLW. The old advice to start solids just once a day, then progress to two and then three meals over a period of a few weeks was aimed at babies starting solids at three or four months of age, whose digestive systems were really too immature for solids. Babies of six months and over are less likely to react badly to new foods, because their gut is more mature. All you need to do at six months is to start to include your baby whenever *you* eat—it could be at breakfast, lunch, dinner or when you have a snack—as long as she isn't tired, or grumpy.

It's also important that your baby isn't hungry when you sit her down to explore food, because in the early weeks of solids, "mealtimes" have nothing to do with hunger and have everything to do with play, sharing, and copying others; they are opportunities to learn rather than to actually eat—they are playtimes. This is very different from conventional weaning methods, when you are generally advised to make sure your baby is hungry at mealtimes. If your baby *is* hungry when you share a meal, she won't be able to enjoy exploring food and developing her self-feeding skills—she'll simply get frustrated and upset, just as she would with a new toy.

> "I can't believe how close I came to giving up BLW in the beginning. Stephanie just didn't seem interested in solids at all—I thought it wasn't working. But one day she was really irritable before lunch, so I gave her a quick breast-feed. I sat her in the high chair and couldn't believe it when she picked up some carrot and started to chew on it! It was only then that I finally realized what I was doing wrong—I just needed to give her the solids when she wasn't hungry."
>
> *Annabel, mother of Zoe, 2,*
> *and Stephanie, 8 months*

Baby-led weaning works best if you are giving your baby her milk feedings whenever she wants them ("on demand"). That way she can carry on taking in as much milk as she needs and enjoy exploring solid foods as a separate activity. Remember, she has no idea yet that solid food can fill her tummy, so, if you think she is getting hungry when you have a meal planned, offer her a milk feeding. If she's too sleepy afterward to be interested in solids, don't worry—you can simply offer her something later, when she is more alert.

It doesn't matter if you miss "meals" at this stage, since your baby won't be relying on them for nourishment (or to stop her being hungry) for another couple of months. So although it's good to give her as many opportunities to practice her feeding skills as you can, there's no need to insist that she joins in every meal, or to feel you have to keep her awake for an evening meal. (Eventually, most parents end up adapting mealtimes to fit in with when their child is hungry—but this probably won't be necessary until she's around a year old—see page 80.)

The interest your baby takes in food will probably be unpredictable from day to day. She may want to eat at every meal for three days and then go back to milk feedings only for the next four. This natural progression of two steps forward, one step back is nothing like the strict timetables that parents are sometimes encouraged to follow. Provided you let your baby stay in control of the process she will build up her intake of solids gradually. That way her body can continue to take in all the breast milk or formula she needs without filling up on foods that are less nutritious, while she adjusts at a pace that is right for *her*.

Tips for getting started

- Offer your baby solids when she's *not* hungry—breast milk or formula is still her main source of nourishment.

- Keep the focus on playing and experimenting.
- Let your baby join in your mealtimes (and snacktimes) whenever possible.
- Make sure your baby is upright and safe in a high chair or on your lap.

Finger Food

The key to BLW in the early months is to offer food that is easy and safe for your baby to pick up and take to her mouth. So although you can let her have almost anything she can grab from your plate (see pages 96–101 for the exceptions), it will be easier for her—and less frustrating—if you include foods of a shape and size that she can manage.

Babies of six months use their whole hand to pick things up; they can't usually pick up small things with their thumb and forefinger until they're a few months older. This means they must be able to close their hand around a piece of food to hold it, so it mustn't be so wide or thick that they can't do this.

Babies of this age also need the food to stick out beyond their palm because they can't open their fist on purpose to get to it. When your baby is first starting, her aim won't be very accurate, so long pieces of food stand a better chance of being picked up than short ones. Sticks or "fingers" of food, at least two inches long, mean that half the length is available for eating while the other half is the handle to hold it with. There's no need to be exact—you'll soon see what your baby can manage. Broccoli is an ideal first food because it already has a "handle"—but all kinds of fruit and vegetables, and most meat, can be cut into a rough finger shape. So, wash your baby's hands and make sure she is sitting up securely, then simply offer her some stick shapes to play with.

If you are offering vegetables, bear in mind they shouldn't be too soft (or they'll turn to mush when your baby tries to handle them) or too hard (or she won't be able to gnaw them easily). See Chapter 4 for more information on how to adapt your food for your baby.

A baby of six or seven months will normally gnaw or munch on the part of the food that sticks out of her fist. She may bite off a small piece and will then probably drop the rest as she goes to pick up something else. This isn't a sign that she doesn't like the food, just that she is not yet able to open her hand on purpose or to concentrate on two things at once. This first stage usually lasts only a couple of months or so; by about eight months your baby will be able to get at food inside her fist and, as her skills develop, you will find she can manage smaller pieces and more awkward shapes and no longer needs the "handle."

"I cut everything into finger shapes at the beginning, but I didn't realize that they weren't quite long enough. Lucy couldn't move her hand down or release the food. There was nothing poking out of her fist to eat. She must have been so frustrated. I just didn't know what she could and couldn't do. I found out some time later that food needed to be long enough to have a 'handle' for her to hold."

Laura, mother of Josie, 10,
and Lucy, 17 months

Improving Coordination

Once babies can pick up pieces of food accurately and are learning to open their fist to get at food inside it they often go through a phase of using two hands to feed themselves. This is all part of their developing coordination. At this stage they often find it easier to reach their mouth if they use their other hand to guide the hand with the food in it. Once your baby figures this out you will probably notice that she "misses" her mouth much less frequently.

In the early stages, some babies also use one or both hands to keep the food in their mouth while they chew it. This is because they haven't yet found out how to open and close their jaws without opening and closing their lips. As soon as your baby has learned to keep her lips closed while chewing she will be able to use her hands to get the next mouthful ready without the first one falling out!

By about nine months your baby will be able to pick up small pieces between her finger and thumb, so she will be able to manage food such as raisins and peas. She will also be able to "dip" fairly accurately, so you can offer her soft foods such as hummus or yogurt to eat with a breadstick, a piece of rice cake, or with her fingers. (If you want to offer runny foods before your baby can "dip" by herself, you can do the dipping for her—with a spoon or piece of food—and then

OUCH!

Sometimes babies put their fingers into their mouth along with the food. This is fine, until they accidentally bite down a bit too hard on a finger! If your baby suddenly cries while eating, this is probably what's happened. Unfortunately, there's nothing you can do to prevent it from happening— it's just something she has to find out for herself. So, until she figures it out, just be ready to give her a quick cuddle and kiss it all better.

simply offer your baby the dipper so she can lick the food off it. See page 113 for more ideas on dips and dippers.)

As long as you offer your baby plenty of food that she *can* pick up, it's good to let her experiment with foods that she is still too young to manage (apart from foods that could be choking hazards such as whole nuts and fruit with pits—see page 96). Handling lots of different textures and shapes will help her develop the skills she needs to eat a varied diet—and she may surprise you with what she can do.

> "Millie has become better at manipulating food now; she'll turn broccoli around so she can eat the floret, because she knows she can eat that bit more easily. She's also worked out how to eat fruit or vegetables and leave the skin."
> *Beth, mother of Millie, 10 months*

> "Bronwyn's getting good now at scooping stuff into her mouth, rather than just holding on to a stick of something. And she picks up little bits, too, and puts her whole hand in her mouth, and drops the food there. Then she has a good suck on her fingers and then her hand comes out for more."
> *Faye, mother of William, 4, and Bronwyn, 7 months*

Offering Rather Than Giving

We often talk about "giving" babies food but all you're really doing with BLW is *offering*—by placing suitable pieces within your baby's reach—either on your plate, or on the tabletop or high chair tray—then letting her decide what to do with it. She may play with it, drop it, smear it, take it to her mouth, or simply sniff it; but it's up to her whether or not she eats it.

It's easy to be tempted to put things into your baby's mouth for her but not only is it more enjoyable for her to be in control, it's also much safer; putting things into a baby's mouth can be a choking hazard (see page 48). It's also important to let her decide whether to pick something up or not, so she can choose what she is going to explore or eat, so try to avoid making these decisions for her by handing her pieces of food. Baby-led weaning works best as a "hands-off" approach—the more you can trust your baby to explore in her own way and in her own time, the faster she'll learn and the more confident she'll become.

Remember to make sure that food isn't too hot before you offer it—tasting is more reliable than touching with your lips or using your finger. A good tip is to put your baby's food on a plate that has been in the fridge for half an hour—this will help it to cool down faster. Your baby is likely to feel left out if she has to wait for her meal to cool down while everyone else is digging into theirs!

How Much Food to Offer

When your baby first starts on solids she'll be eating very little and playing a lot. For the first few weeks pretty much all the food you give her will end up in the chair or on the floor, mainly because babies can take food to their mouths and gnaw it before they're able to swallow it. This means that, even if it gets as far as her mouth, it will probably come out again. In the early days, she may lose interest or get tired quite quickly, or she may want to play for ages but eat very little. Many babies like to take their time, trying out different pieces of food, moving on, and then coming back to them. All this is normal.

MICROWAVE HOTSPOTS

If you microwave food, be sure to turn or stir it while it's cooking—and remember to test the temperature before you offer any to your baby. It is safer to test microwaved food by taking a sample mouthful than by feeling the food with your lips because microwaving can heat food unevenly, producing unexpected hotspots.

Remember that, at this stage, she can still get all the nourishment she needs from breast milk or formula.

Even when she does begin to swallow small amounts your baby will still spread, smear, and drop a lot of food. Some of this will be on purpose—as a key part of her learning—and some will be by mistake, because she is simply not mature enough to hold on to it.

Offer your baby three or four different things to start with— maybe a piece of carrot, a broccoli floret and a large strip of meat (or whatever you happen to be eating that's suitable). Be prepared to have some more food ready to offer her, or to pick up the food she has dropped and pass it back to her. It's tempting to restrict your baby to just one piece of food at her first few meals, on the grounds that she isn't going to eat it anyway. But this will be boring for her—and you'll find yourself having to pick the food up and hand it back to her every two minutes. It's much better to provide a small selection of foods and not worry about whether she eats it or not.

On the other hand, it's not a good plan to pile your baby's tray high with lots of different foods, either. It's better to start with a small amount and then offer more. Many babies can be overwhelmed by too much choice and too much quantity in the early stages. Some push all the food away; others focus on one piece of food and throw everything else off the high chair tray; some simply turn away. Watch how your baby responds to food to see how much she can cope with at first.

> "When we first started I'd give Etta a plate with lots of food on it, and she'd do this really funny thing: she'd pick up almost every single bit and throw it all behind her until she had just one thing left. She would then grasp it carefully in her hand and start eating. And when she'd eaten it, she'd look around for more. But I couldn't just refill her plate because it'd all go down again. It was as if there was just too much in front of her and she found it confusing. Eventually I worked out that all I had to do was put her food on another plate, and then just offer it to her one or two pieces at a time."
>
> Julie, mother of Etta, 3

As your baby's self-feeding skills develop, you will find that less food is dropped and more is eaten, and you may get a sense of how much she is likely to eat at mealtimes. But beware! It's only a small step from this to deciding how much she "should" eat, and this is not what BLW is all about. Encouraging a child to eat more than she needs is unnecessary, and may even be harmful in the long term. At best, it may spoil her enjoyment of mealtimes and at worst it could make her more likely to overeat when she's older. It should always be your baby's decision how much she eats; it's her tummy and she knows what she needs.

Tip

Don't give your baby too much food at once—but have more available than you think she'll need, just so you don't run out before she loses interest. If you give a child less than you think she "should" eat, the chances are she won't leave much—and she'll soon let you know if she needs more. Even if she doesn't, there's a much better chance you'll feel good about how much she's eaten.

Having a Clean Plate

Although many of us have grown up being told that it's good manners to finish whatever is on our plates and not to waste food, neither of these things really works for babies or children—and they are often associated with overeating in adults. So it's important not to expect your baby to eat everything she's been given, or try to persuade her to eat more than she wants. She should be allowed to eat as much (or as little) as she wants from the food you offer her, so she can choose the nutrients she needs. If she eats everything you've given her, by all means offer her some more (or something different) just to make sure she really has had enough; if she turns it down it's her way of saying she's full. Even though she may have eaten less than you think she should have, she doesn't need you to "top her off" with something from a spoon; she may well take it to please you—but that doesn't mean she needed it.

> "I grew up in London during the war, when there was rationing. You couldn't afford to waste food. If I didn't eat up everything I was given I got it served up again at the next meal. That feeling of needing to finish the plateful (even if I didn't like it) has stayed with me all my life."
>
> *Tony, father of three and grandfather of five*

Rejecting Food

If your baby rejects a certain food it's because she doesn't need it (or want it) *at that particular time*. It's not a reflection on your cooking, and it doesn't mean she won't eat it if you offer it again. Of course, if your baby is eating the same food as everyone else, rather than a specially prepared dish, you are much less likely to even notice how much she's eaten—this is another reason why sharing your food with her is less stressful for you both than preparing her food separately.

Tips for offering your baby food

- Wash your baby's hands before she handles food.
- Offer pieces of food that are stick-shaped and at least two inches long—half to hold and half to munch.
- Make sure your baby is the one who decides what goes into her mouth—put food within easy reach (on her high chair tray or the tabletop).
- Check that the food is not too hot (testing a mouthful yourself is more reliable than using your finger).
- Offer your baby a small selection of foods to start with. Overloading her could put her off.
- Have more food ready in case she wants it.
- Remember that "a clean plate" isn't what you're aiming for—it's important for your baby to eat only as much as she needs.
- Don't be offended if she doesn't eat the food you've prepared.
- Always stay with your baby when she is eating or playing with food.

Occasionally babies tuck away a piece of food—usually in their cheek—only to produce it later. This generally happens before they've worked out how to use their tongue to retrieve bits that have become lodged between their gum and their cheek. To be on the safe side it's probably a good idea, once the meal is over, to check that this hasn't happened before your baby starts playing or has a nap. There's no need to poke around inside her mouth or pin her down to have a good look—just make a game of asking her to open her mouth wide (perhaps by getting her to copy you), or, once she can understand a bit more, teach her to check with her own finger that nothing is lurking inside.

Helping Your Baby to Learn

Babies learn by copying, and they love to join in, so it's important that you eat with your baby whenever possible and offer her some of the same food that you are eating. In fact, you may find she prefers what's on your plate to what's on her own anyway, even if it is exactly the same! (This is probably her instinctive way of checking that the food is safe, see page 21.) Talk to her about the different foods, naming them and describing their colors and textures, so that she learns new words at the same time as she is developing new skills.

"Meena knows what a piece of carrot is; it's not just orange mush. We talk about the food, and she's getting

to know the names of different vegetables. I'll say,
'Where's the cauliflower?' and she'll pick it up. It's great.
Babies don't have the chance to learn about real food
when you mush it all up into a purée."

Deepti, mother of Meena, 10 months

Learning by copying involves watching and then doing—and making mistakes. It's important to let your baby find her own way to manage food and not to give her more help than she actually needs. Helping too much (or interfering), criticizing her, laughing at her or being cross with her will confuse her and may stop her trying. On the other hand, she doesn't need to be praised when she "gets it right," either. After all, she doesn't see a dropped piece of food as a "failure" or food eaten as a "success"—to her it's all just an interesting part of the experiment.

Trying to help or guide your baby can also be very distracting for her. Remember, she is concentrating on learning about food and how to eat it. If she needs your help she'll let you know. Most babies really do just want to work out how to do it on their own.

"At first, Jamal would be in the process of picking something up and we would reach over to help him when he couldn't quite manage—but you could see his concentration breaking the minute we did it. He was much happier if we just let him do it himself."

Simon, father of Jamal, 8 months

You may find your baby gags occasionally in the early days while she is learning how to manage food. Although this may look alarming, it is unlikely to worry her, and there's no need to try and stop it from happening. In fact it may play an important part in her learning, teaching her how to eat safely by not pushing food too far back or overfilling her mouth (see page 46). She'll naturally stop gagging after practicing for a few weeks, because she'll have learned how to avoid it.

If you think of these first experiences not as mealtimes (for eating) but as opportunities for playing and learning, you will see that there is no reason to limit them to one, two, or even three a day, or to stick to a particular schedule. In fact, the more opportunities your baby has to explore food and to practice with it, the more quickly she will discover what it's all about and develop the self-feeding skills she'll need later.

Dealing with Frustration

Some babies seem to go through a period shortly after they start exploring solids when they seem frustrated; it's as though their skills aren't developing fast enough for them. It's tempting to assume that a baby who gets upset and cross is frustrated because she is hungry—but in the early weeks if she *is* hungry it is almost certainly for a milk feeding, not for solids. So a baby's frustration isn't a sign that she can't get enough solid food and she doesn't need her parents to "help" her by mashing the solids up and spooning them into her; milk is still sufficient to meet her needs. Giving food off a spoon may appear to solve the problem but only because the baby is temporarily distracted. If she is hungry or tired it's better to offer her a milk feeding, or encourage her to have a nap.

Babies can also get frustrated in the first few weeks of BLW simply because they can't do everything they would like to be able to do with the food—in the same way that a new toy can be challenging. Often the problem is that the food is not the right shape or is too slippery for them to grasp, so it's important to watch for this (see page 66 on ways to prepare food so that it's easy to hold). The good news is that, although a period of frustration seems to be quite common among BLW babies, it rarely lasts more than a week or so, in the same way that being frustrated with a new toy doesn't last forever.

Allowing Enough Time

Babies need to take their time when they are learning, so it's important not to rush them. It could easily take your baby 40 minutes to "finish" a meal in the early days—it's all about her needing to practice each new skill over and over again before she manages to get it "right."

It's especially important to allow babies time to chew thoroughly because this helps with digestion and may prevent tummy ache and constipation. If you let your baby eat at her own pace she will also learn to recognize when she is full. (See also pages 44–45—eating too fast has been linked to obesity in older children and adults.)

Some babies like to leave pieces of food while they explore other things, but they may want to come back to them later. This "grazing" habit is quite common, so try to resist the temptation to start cleaning up too soon or nibbling at your baby's food yourself.

Standing back and letting your baby explore may be the hardest part of BLW, but if you can be relaxed about it you'll soon find this stage doesn't last forever. In fact, the more time you give your baby to learn how to deal with food—and to sniff it, feel it, and play with it—the more quickly she'll become a confident and skilled eater.

"Ivor will happily feed himself in his own time. Sometimes he'll sit there for a long time and not do much, and then

suddenly eat quite a bit. And some days he'll eat loads
and then have nothing but milk for a few days. We really
have to trust him and not interfere."

Amanda, mother of Ivor, 8 months

No Pressure

Some babies can be discouraged from trying foods if they
are made to feel self-conscious or under pressure by their
parents (or others) watching every mouthful they eat. Try not
to pay too much attention to your baby while she's eating; you
may be fascinated to watch, but she won't feel comfortable
being stared at. Mealtimes should be a normal, enjoyable,
everyday activity. Your quiet support and the rewards of
handling and eating food are all she needs to grow in skill and
confidence.

"I remember having dinner with friends when Enrico was
about seven or eight months, and they were just staring
at him eating—they seemed really anxious. I could tell it
was really off-putting for him but I guess it was just all
new to them."   *Angela, mother of Enrico, 2*

Eating Together

Eating together as a family is ideal, because your child will
learn about more than just how to handle food. She'll learn
about taking turns, conversation, and table manners (see page
163). Organizing mealtimes for a busy family can be a real
challenge—especially when one partner (or both) works long
hours outside the home. However, the most important thing is

that, as far as possible, your baby shouldn't be the only one eating. So, even if a family meal isn't possible, try to make sure that she always eats with at least one other person. If your baby is cared for by someone else, explaining this to a grandparent, day care provider, or nanny will help to make sure that she experiences shared mealtimes even when she isn't with you.

Breakfast can be rushed in many households, especially if both parents work or there are older children that you need to get to school. Many babies won't be interested in breakfast in the early days, but once they are, they tend to be very adaptable: they don't mind if it's not the "right" time to eat. So your baby could have breakfast after the school drop-off or when she's at day care. If you're not at work, lunch is probably the easiest meal to share with your baby at first. It doesn't have to be anything elaborate, as long as it's nutritious and has a bit of variety in it (see page 187 for ideas).

Shared evening meals are often the most difficult to manage for families, especially where parents work long days. Often the main caregiver (usually the mother) ends up eating two meals; one with the baby and then another when her partner comes home from work.

You may find you can rethink your baby's bedtime (if it's very early) or change your evening mealtime, if it's very late. Bear in mind that your baby doesn't need her solid "meals" at regular times in the early days, because she's not relying on them to satisfy her hunger. It's only as she begins to eat more and discovers that food can stop her hunger that you'll start to see a pattern in her eating; this is when you can begin to plan how to make family meals coincide with her needs.

Shared meals are probably best around a table, but they don't have to be. If you normally eat dinner on your lap in front of the TV, just turn the TV off (so your baby can concentrate) and pull her chair up beside you. Or why not eat together on a mat or rug on the floor, either indoors or outside?

Aim to treat your baby with the same respect you would any other mealtime companion. That means not telling her what to eat or how much, not constantly wiping her face, and resisting the temptation to do the washing-up while she is still eating!

> "Leah will eat and chew better when I'm eating at the table with her. She watches me the whole time and copies my chewing action. Occasionally I'll get up and start doing something else, and she definitely loses her focus."
>
> *Emily, mother of Leah, 7 months*

Tips

- As far as possible, aim to eat the same food as your baby, with your baby.
- Allow your baby plenty of time to explore the food and decide what she wants to do with it.
- Talk to your baby about the food she is exploring.
- Resist the temptation to help your baby eat more than she really needs.
- Allow your baby to handle food as much as possible to help her develop her skills.
- Share your baby's enjoyment as she makes discoveries but remember that there's no need to direct her learning by praising or scolding her.

BLW STORY

Once Owen could sit up properly I sat him on my lap at the table with us; he was just over six months. He picked pieces of food up right away but he missed his mouth nearly all the time at first—I don't think he got anything at all for a few days.

But his hand-eye coordination and the way he can get things to his mouth have really changed, even though he only started a couple of weeks ago. The first thing I gave him was some pear—that's what the other kids were eating—and every time he grabbed it, the pear just kept slipping out of his hand; he didn't get any of it. The next time he had pear he kept squeezing it until he eventually worked out the tension he needed to keep it in his hand. After that he started to work out that if he picks up something in his left hand it's easier to pass it to his right hand to get it to his mouth, and now he's started to use his left hand to help to guide it—the left hand pushes the right hand closer to his mouth. It's fascinating.

Actually *eating* stuff still seems to be a bit of a fluke. Food seems to be for the experience of tasting and experimenting rather than for eating at the moment.

It feels great being able to trust my baby's instincts. He doesn't always want food; at dinnertime he's often too tired to be interested, and sometimes I don't give him much at breakfast if I'm late getting the others to school; I'm fairly relaxed with it. But there's no way I could sit and have a meal now and not include him—I'm really enjoying it.

Sharing normal family meals with Owen makes sense to me; it's so much easier than when I did purées with my first two. In hindsight, Theo (my second) wasn't ready for food until he was about seven months. He didn't like soft food, and he didn't like being fed—he would just spit it all out. He really didn't want to eat much until he was allowed to feed himself. It just seems more natural to let them do that from the start.

Sam, mother of Ella, 8, Theo, 5, and Owen, 8 months

Expect Mess

Babies don't understand the concept of mess. Your baby will drop or throw her toys all the time; it's how she learns about gravity, distance, and her own strength. Food is just another toy at first, so babies experiment with it in the same way. To their delight, they find that nothing they have handled so far can be squished and spread in quite this way (messy play and play dough are usually reserved for older babies in case the little ones eat it!)

Sometimes the mess is just because young babies' skills are still immature. They often knock something over or push it to one side as they try to pick it up. And because they aren't able to open their fists consciously at first, they tend to drop things by accident when their interest is taken by something else. The most important thing to remember when you are watching your baby merrily lobbing food over the edge of her high chair is that *she doesn't know it matters!* She doesn't know that it needs to be cleaned up—she is just engaged in the important activity of learning. The more relaxed you can be, the quicker she will learn.

As your baby's skills develop and she discovers the delights of actually eating the food you offer her, the mess will quickly get less. In fact, parents who've taken a baby-led approach to weaning often comment on how short-lived the messy stage was and how quickly their baby's skills developed in comparison with those of other babies. It's also worth remembering that, while BLW may be more messy than spoon-feeding during the meals themselves, it's much less messy (and less time-consuming) during the preparation phase, with no blenders or sieves to clean.

Mess is an inevitable and important part of babies' learning—trying to fight it is like standing on the seashore and asking the tide not to come in! The secret to coping with the mess is to welcome it and prepare for it in advance. This means thinking about how you will dress your baby (and yourself!) for her self-feeding adventures and about how best to protect the area around her. It also means allowing plenty of time for meals, giving your baby lots of opportunities to practice (so she can learn to eat less messily), and allowing plenty of time for cleanup.

> "Mealtimes have been Milo's messy play. He's learned about texture and volume and pouring things through handling food, and it's really helped with hand-eye coordination. Kids love playing with messy stuff. At day care you see kids playing with big trays of colored jelly or cooked spaghetti—but not for their dinner. It's their playtime! It's cutting-edge early learning. Amazing, isn't it?"
>
> *Helen, mother of Lizzie, 7, Saul, 5, and Milo, 2*

Bibs

Unlike you, your baby won't be sitting above her food, and she may need to reach out the whole length of her arms to grab what she wants. Long sleeves are likely to get covered in food—and may get in her way—so short sleeves (or rolled-up sleeves) are better. A bib will help to protect her front—a long-sleeved one (or a toddler's painting apron) will cover her arms too but, again, may get in the way. "Pelican" bibs are useful for catching dropped food, but they tend to restrict a young baby's movements, so are perhaps not a good idea at first.

Some parents prefer to let their baby eat in an undershirt—or even just in a diaper, if it's warm enough; skin is easier to wash than clothes. (If your baby has a regular bathtime, make sure it's *after* she's eaten!) As with high chairs (see page 86), it's not worth battling if your baby doesn't like bibs—mealtimes should be enjoyable. Accept that your baby will probably get food on her face, in her hair, and on her clothes and that nothing has yet been invented that will stop food from finding its way onto the seat of a high chair or onto the floor. In fact, you'll be amazed at where you find bits of food once your baby has finished experimenting with her meal.

FRUIT STAINS

Watch out for fruit stains. When babies eat fruit (especially whole fruit) they tend to suck and munch for ages and the juice or pulp often dribbles down their chin and hands and onto their clothes. You may not notice it at the time but some fruits, such as banana and apple, can leave very dark stains.

"I really took to 1950s-style aprons when Justin started BLW, and I haven't looked back. If the baby sits on your lap at mealtimes you get covered—aprons take all the mess!" *Louise, mother of Justin, 23 months*

"After the meal you start with a clean damp cloth: you clean the baby's face, the baby's hands, and you put him somewhere clean. Then you flip the cloth around and you clean the table: you sweep all the food down on to the floor, then you clean the high chair and sweep all the bits on to the floor. So you've got a big pile on the floor—basically the remains of the entire dinner. You sweep it all up with the cloth, put it into the trash, then put the cloth in the wash. One cloth per meal. Everything's done."

Hazel, mother of Hannah, 8, Nathan, 4,
and Joe, 17 months

Protecting the floor

Carpets can be protected by a large "splash mat" that's kept clean, so that any food that gets dropped (or thrown) can be given back to the baby. A plastic or cotton tablecloth or picnic blanket will do fine. Some parents just use newspaper, which can be thrown away after the meal, so that they don't have to spend time cleaning. Some also invest in a hand vacuum to keep nearby for quick cleanups.

> "We tried a splash mat, but the plastic was fairly thin so we couldn't just mop it to get it clean, we'd have to be down on our hands and knees. In the end we decided to use a cheap cotton tablecloth—then we could just shake it over the trash after a meal and shove it in the washing machine. We ended up needing two or three, so there was always a clean one, but there's always so much washing with a baby it didn't seem to make any difference."
>
> *Ruth, mother of Lola, 19 months*

Equipment

High chairs

High chairs come in all sorts of shapes and sizes. A high chair with a tray may be useful early on but one that can be used with the main table will usually save space and, most important, make your child feel part of the family meal. One that can be pulled up close to the table will make it easier for your baby to reach the food. A small cushion or rolled-up towel behind her may be useful.

If you opt for a high chair with a tray, aim for a very wide tray; this usually means less food ends up on the floor. And choose one with a rim around the edge—a tray with no lip may look good, but the food won't stay on it very long. It's also important to make sure the tray isn't too high in relation to the seat: if your baby's chest is level with the tray she won't be able to reach the food easily (imagine trying to eat off a table that came up to your armpits!) High chairs with an adjustable-height tray are good, but, if you haven't got one, putting a folded towel under your baby's bottom will help her until she grows a bit.

High chairs that clamp on to the table can be useful for eating out or traveling, but probably aren't comfortable enough for everyday use. Some high chairs can also be used in a low position, which may be handy if you don't eat at a standard table. Chairs that can be adjusted as your child grows are expensive initially but will save you having to buy a booster seat or a stool when your baby is a toddler. Some can even be adjusted and used as a normal chair for older children or adults.

Beware of high chairs with lots of padding—they may look more comfortable than plain wood or plastic, but they are much more difficult to clean. And, honestly, you *will* need to clean it.

It's important that your baby's high chair has straps to secure her—and that you use them every time she's in it; she may not be trying to climb out yet, but accidents can happen when babies wriggle around.

High chairs are handy, long-term, but if your baby isn't happy in one, don't force her—she'll be able to eat just as well on your lap, and she'll probably come around to a high chair eventually.

"If I had another baby I wouldn't do mealtimes any differently—except maybe forget about the high chair! It's so recently that Aidan's sat in a high chair without a fuss—and he's two. So we just decided not to bother because he didn't like it. I just accepted that he would be on my lap, rather than have a fight over it. It can be hard to cut food up when he's squirming around, but apart from that, we enjoy it."

Sue, mother of Aidan, 2

Plates

Many parents find that it's easier not to bother with a plate at first. A baby of six months is likely to be just as interested in the plate as the food—especially if it's a colorful plate designed for babies—and, while this doesn't really matter, it will probably mean that any food on the plate quickly ends up on the floor. And your baby won't remember to put pieces of food back on to the plate after she has tried them, so the area around it will have food on it anyway.

There is no reason why your baby can't eat straight off her high chair tray, or off the tabletop, as long as it's clean (a quick wipe with a mild detergent and a clean cloth is probably all you need). Alternatively, you could put a large straight-sided kitchen tray on the table in front of her (perhaps held down with sticky pads) or a rubber placemat with a built-in pocket to catch food that drops down. These help to contain the mess and are easy to clean.

If you do want to use a plate you may find that a heavy bowl or plate will be less easy for your baby to lift up—although it will do more damage if she does manage it. Suction plates that stick to the table can be useful but they tend to catapult out any food left in them when *you* pick them up! Any plates, bowls and cups you *do* use should be clean, but they don't need to be sterilized.

BLW STORY

About a month ago James started making it clear that he wanted to sit at the table with us—he wasn't content to sit and watch our mealtimes from a bouncy chair anymore. Some people say when they're interested at mealtimes, they're ready to eat, but I don't think he was hungry. He just wanted to join in, in the same way that he gets frustrated and wants to copy when he sees other babies crawling.

At first he was interested in things *to do* with mealtimes, but not actually the food. That's really changed in the last two weeks. He's sitting really sturdily now, and he wants more than just a spoon to play with or something nice to suck—he wants to grab things.

He grabbed a piece of cucumber a few weeks ago, but he still couldn't hold things well, and he dropped it. The other kids are naughty; they want to give him food. He was given a carrot stick, and a piece of banana, and a mouthful of yogurt by his brother. He managed to grab an apple core to suck on when we went on a picnic the other day—he was very happy with that. And I've had a tomato-y finger that he's sucked on. So he's enjoying tastes. It feels to me like he's ready to eat now.

So, today, I actually offered him something for the first time. It was a nice ripe pear—and he really loved it. I think he was very glad to finally be allowed to eat what he wanted to eat, rather than me saying, "Oh, no, you're not old enough yet."

Last night I made a chicken and bean stew, and I was thinking, "How would this work with James?" But I guess he would maybe have to scoop some up with his hands, or grab pieces of chicken. It would be a terrible mess, and I'd just have to get used to it! I think that's my challenge: "What can he eat that isn't too different?"

Jane, mother of Rose, 7, Edward, 3, and James, 6 months

If you want to protect your tabletop you may want to invest in a plastic or oilcloth tablecloth. These are useful because they are very easy to clean, but it's best to choose one without a "busy" or colorful pattern, since that can make it harder for your baby to see and recognize the food. It's also important to make sure she can't pull the tablecloth (and everything on it) into her lap or on to the floor.

The Secrets of Successful BLW

- *Think of mealtimes as playtimes in the beginning.* They are for learning and experimenting—not necessarily eating. Your baby will still be getting all her nourishment from breast milk or formula.

- *Keep giving milk feedings on demand,* so that your baby's solid foods add to them rather than replace them. She will reduce them gradually, in her own time.

- *Don't expect your baby to eat much food at first.* She doesn't suddenly need extra food just because she has reached six months. As she discovers that food tastes nice she will begin to chew, and later to swallow. Many babies eat very little for the first few months.

- *Try to eat with your baby and include her in your meals whenever possible,* so that she has plenty of opportunities to copy you and practice her new skills.

- *Expect some mess!* Think about how to dress your baby and how to protect the area around her so that dealing with the mess isn't stressful and dropped food can be safely handed back. Remember, she's learning, not trying to make work for you.

Keep it enjoyable—for all of you. By making sure that meal-times are always relaxed and enjoyable you will encourage your baby to explore and experiment. That way she'll be keen to try new foods and look forward to mealtimes.

Six things you should do

1. *Ensure that your baby is supported in an upright position while she is experimenting with food.* In the early days you can sit her on your lap, facing the table. Once she is in a high chair, use small cushions or rolled-up towels to keep her upright and at the right level with the tray or table.

2. *Start by offering foods that are easy to pick up.* Thick sticks are easiest. As far as possible (provided they are suitable) offer your baby the same foods that you are eating, so that she feels part of what is going on. Don't forget that a young baby can't get at food in her fist, so don't expect her to eat all of each piece—and be ready to offer her more if she's eaten the bit that sticks out.

3. *Offer a variety of foods.* There is no need to limit your baby's experience with food. While it's important not to overload her at each meal, offering her plenty of different tastes and textures throughout the week will provide her with a wide range of nutri-ents, as well as help her to develop her eating skills.

4. *Continue to offer your baby breast milk or formula as you did before* and offer her water with her meals (see page 148). Expect her milk-feeding pattern to change only very gradually as she starts to eat more.

5. *Discuss the introduction of solids with your pediatrician if* you have a family history of food intolerance, allergies, or digestive problems or any other concerns about your baby's health or development.

6. *Explain how BLW works to anyone caring for your baby.*

Six things you shouldn't do

1. *Don't offer your baby foods that aren't good for her*, such as "fast" foods, prepackaged meals, or foods that have added salt or sugar. Keep foods that present an obvious danger of choking out of her reach.

2. *Don't offer your baby solid food when she is hungry for milk.*

3. *Don't hurry your baby or distract her while she is handling food*—allow her to concentrate and direct the pace of what she is doing.

4. *Don't put food into your baby's mouth for her* (and watch out for "helpful" toddlers who may try this, too). Letting the baby stay in control is an important safety feature of BLW.

5. *Don't try to persuade your baby to eat more than she wants.* There is no need for coaxing, bribing, threatening, or games.

6. *NEVER leave your baby alone with food.*

Q&A

My baby is five months old, and I've been giving her puréed food for a month now. Can I change to BLW?

At five months your baby is almost certainly still too young to feed herself with solid food, although she may be able to pick some pieces up and get them to her lips. But unless you started solids early for a medical reason (in which case you should ask your pediatrician for advice) she doesn't really need solids at this age anyway. It might be better to let her go back to full milk feedings for a few more weeks until her system is more mature.

If you don't want your baby to stop having solid foods, you will need to continue giving her puréed food until she's able to feed herself. If, however, you want to revert to truly *baby-led* weaning, then it would be best to go back to feeding your baby milk alone until she is six months old and then start with finger foods—just as if she had never had the purées. In order to do this, you'll need to increase her milk feedings now (by feeding her more often, if you are breast-feeding, or by increasing the quantity of each feeding if you are formula-feeding) so that you can stop the puréed food.

My baby is eight months old and I've been giving her purées up till now. Is it too late to start BLW?

It's never too late to start BLW! Even if your baby is used to being spoon-fed, she will probably still enjoy exploring food if she's given the chance, and she'll still benefit from it, but she may respond slightly differently from babies who have fed themselves from the beginning.

When babies start with BLW at six months they have a chance to experiment with food and develop self-feeding skills while all their nutrition is still coming from breast milk or formula. This means they can practice feeding themselves before they really need much food. But if they start weaning with a period of spoon-feeding and then move on to BLW, progress may be less straightforward because this opportunity has been missed.

You may find, when you first offer your baby finger food, that she gets frustrated because she can't feed herself as fast as she wants to. Babies who have been spoon-fed can get used to swallowing large quantities of food quickly when they are hungry because puréed food doesn't need to be chewed.

Giving your baby the chance to feed herself when she *isn't* hungry can help you both avoid this problem by allowing her to concentrate on discovering that food can be fun without thinking about filling her tummy. Start to offer finger foods at her mealtimes, too, alongside her usual purée and, as she begins to develop her self-feeding skills, you'll find she is less interested in the purées you offer her, and there is eventually no need for them.

Some parents find that older babies who are used to being spoon-fed try to cram too much into their mouths when they are allowed to feed themselves. This may be because they haven't had a chance to get used to chewing food before swallowing it, or possibly because they haven't been able to discover (through their gag reflex) how to avoid overfilling their mouths (see page 46). Encouraging self-feeding when your baby isn't hungry is a good way to help her learn not to do this.

However old your baby is when you start BLW, try to give her the chance to join in whenever anyone else is eating. That way she will be encouraged to copy other people and discover the social side of mealtimes. If she is over a year you may want to give her her own baby-sized cutlery, so that she can copy what you do. If necessary, just continue to give her the occasional spoonful of puréed food until her self-feeding skills catch up with her appetite.

4.

First Foods

"Within two and a half weeks [of starting BLW], my partner
and I sat at the dinner table, eating homemade vegetarian lasagna and peas, as our daughter sat next to
us—eating the exact same meal and devouring it with
gusto. Was she plastered in it by the end? Yes. Was her
high chair filthy? Yes. Was it one of the most amazing
things I've ever witnessed? Definitely."

Lisa, mother of Kyla, 11 months

Basic Principles

If you have read any other guides to starting solid foods, you
have probably found that most give strict instructions for the
order in which foods should be introduced. However, much of
this advice applies to when solids are given to babies from four,
or even three, months of age. In reality, the immune and digestive systems of a six-month-old baby are much more mature, so
unless there are allergies in the family (or you have other
reasons to suspect allergies) such restrictions are unnecessary.
This is true whether or not a baby-led approach is used.

As a general rule, your meals will be fine for your baby to eat if you start with natural ingredients, serve as much fresh food as possible and cook without adding salt or sugar. Many people begin with plain steamed vegetables or fruit but, although these are probably easiest for your baby to handle initially, there's no reason why he can't share a casserole, salad, pasta dish, stir fry, or roast dinner—or anything else that can include suitable shapes. You should offer:

- nutritious food—not highly processed or with added sugar or salt
- food from each of the major food groups at least once a day (see page 185) (although this is less important while he is just exploring, rather than eating)
- a wide range of foods throughout the week so that your baby gets the chance to sample different tastes and textures
- sizes and shapes that your baby can manage (bearing in mind that his skills will quickly progress)

You can find more detail on nutrients and providing healthy, balanced meals for the whole family in Chapter 7, and once you see your baby handling food you'll realize just how easily you can adapt your meals so that he can join in.

Foods to Avoid

Choking hazards

Some foods are particularly risky for babies and children because of their shape. Nuts are the most well-known example—**whole nuts (or large pieces) should be avoided until**

your child is at least three years old because they can easily get lodged in a small child's windpipe. Fruits such as cherries should have the pits removed before they are offered to your baby and it is also a good idea to cut small round fruits, such as grapes and cherry tomatoes, in half lengthwise. Remember to take care with cakes, casseroles, and salads that may contain small, hard pieces of food. Bony fish is best avoided, too, and gristle should be removed from meat.

Salt

Salt is bad for babies; their kidneys are not mature enough to deal with it, and too much can cause severe illness. It's also better for your baby's long-term health if you can keep salt levels low for him as a child, so he doesn't develop a taste for salty food as he gets older.

Salt is added to many foods to enhance the flavor, especially prepackaged meals and shop-bought sauces, stocks, and gravies, and it is used as a preservative in foods such as bacon and ham and many canned foods. In fact, most of the salt we eat is "hidden" in our food, not added from the saltshaker during cooking or at the table, so avoiding salt means having to think about what you buy as well as how you cook.

Babies up to a year old should have no more than 1 gram of salt (0.4 grams of sodium) per day. Prepackaged meals and processed foods often contain levels of salt that are far too high for babies. Even some cheeses, such as Parmesan, feta, and processed cheese (slices, spread, and triangles) can contain over 1 gram of salt per 100 grams of cheese (although a baby is very unlikely to eat this much cheese in a day!) and some breads can contain 1 gram of salt in a couple of slices. So although cheese and bread can be good foods, they shouldn't be given to babies at every meal.

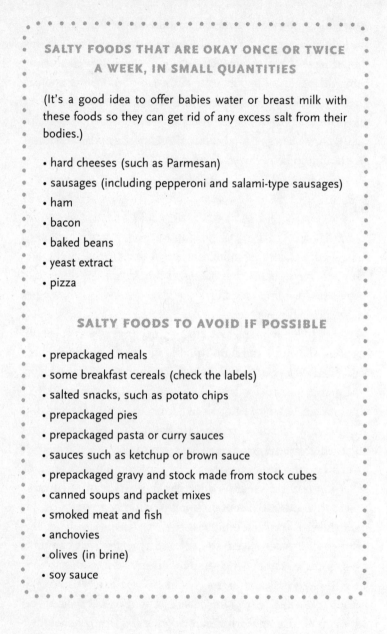

SALTY FOODS THAT ARE OKAY ONCE OR TWICE A WEEK, IN SMALL QUANTITIES

(It's a good idea to offer babies water or breast milk with these foods so they can get rid of any excess salt from their bodies.)

- hard cheeses (such as Parmesan)
- sausages (including pepperoni and salami-type sausages)
- ham
- bacon
- baked beans
- yeast extract
- pizza

SALTY FOODS TO AVOID IF POSSIBLE

- prepackaged meals
- some breakfast cereals (check the labels)
- salted snacks, such as potato chips
- prepackaged pies
- prepackaged pasta or curry sauces
- sauces such as ketchup or brown sauce
- prepackaged gravy and stock made from stock cubes
- canned soups and packet mixes
- smoked meat and fish
- anchovies
- olives (in brine)
- soy sauce

As with all foods, it's worth reading labels carefully when buying. Some manufacturers list salt as "sodium"; multiplying the amount of sodium listed by 2.5 will tell you the equivalent in salt. As a general guide, a food is high in salt if it has more than 1.5 grams of salt (0.6 grams sodium) per 100 grams, while a low-salt food has 0.3 grams or less of salt per 100 grams.

Many parents choose to prepare their own food without salt when they have a young baby, so that the baby can join in their meals without risk. Often they find they can "unlearn" their own preference for salty foods quite quickly, just by changing what they eat and the way they cook. Using herbs and spices can sometimes satisfy the need for highly flavored food and many parents are surprised to find that their baby likes the taste of spicy food—but you may want to avoid hot chili peppers in the early days!

Salt can be added at the table to most dishes by the grown-ups, but bear in mind that, as your baby gets older, he'll start wanting to copy everything you do—so one day he may make a grab for the salt and pour some on to *his* food.

Sugar

Sugar is added to many foods as a sweetener but it doesn't contain any key nutrients, so it provides only "empty calories." It also damages teeth—even before they come through. Starting your baby off on foods that are naturally low in sugar should help to prevent him craving highly sweetened foods later.

There is no need to aim for a totally sugar-free diet for your baby—the occasional cake, cookie, or pudding is fine. But candy and sodas have no real nutritional value, so are best avoided. Even some commercially prepared "baby foods" have high levels of sugar, and it is often "hidden" in products such as sauces, breakfast cereals, flavored yogurts, and baked beans. Watch out for names such as sucrose, dextrose, fructose, glucose syrup, and corn syrup on packets and labels—they are all types of sugar.

You can often reduce the amount of sugar you use when cooking at home by adapting recipes—for example, using naturally sweet eating apples instead of cooking apples to make an apple pie, or adding mashed banana to sweeten dishes. Halving the amount of sugar in many recipes makes no difference to whether or not the recipe "works."

Other unsuitable foods

It's probably best to avoid as many additives and artificial preservatives and sweeteners as possible—monosodium gluta-mate (MSG), aspartame, etc. Generally, the fewer ingredients listed on a packaged food the better it is. But it's always best to cook with fresh ingredients if you can.

Some pediatricians continue to advise against giving babies egg whites until eight months, but others are comfortable with introducing them at six months. Eggs should be cooked thoroughly (including the yolk) because they may contain salmonella, which can cause a serious stomach infection.

Raw honey is best left until your baby is at least a year old as it has been shown to be a potential source of botulism—another serious infection.

Raw bran and bran products (often sold as "high-fiber" cereals) can irritate the digestive tract and interfere with the absorption of essential nutrients such as iron and calcium; they shouldn't be given to babies.

Peanut butter and other products containing nuts are best left until your baby is at least two, if not older. You may like to consult your pediatrician before introducing your child to peanut butter. Whole nuts themselves should not be given until a child is at least three, as they present a choking hazard.

Tuna, while a rich source of Omega-3s for baby, also tends to be high in mercury levels. Babies should have no more than two servings per week (or one portion of albacore "white" tuna).

Drinks

Apart from their normal milk feedings, babies don't need any drinks other than breast milk or water (see page 148 for more on drinks). It's especially important to avoid the following:

- *Coffee, tea, and cola drinks.* These all contain caffeine, which is a stimulant and can make babies irritable. Tea also interferes with iron absorption.

- *Sweetened drinks and undiluted fruit juices.* These have a high sugar content and tend to be very acidic.

- *Milk.* Animal milks are very filling and they risk cutting down a baby's appetite for breast- or formula-feedings. They shouldn't be given as a drink to children under a year old (although they can be used in cooking or with cereals from six months on).

Apart from these foods and drinks, your baby can have anything that you are eating. If you don't suspect any allergies in your family, just offer him a balanced selection of foods—preferably what you're eating yourself—and let him choose what to eat. In fact, the greater the range of tastes and textures he is allowed to try (and to refuse) when he is young, the more likely he is to enjoy a wide range of good foods later.

Allergy Triggers

By waiting until six months to introduce solid foods, you are already helping to reduce your child's risk of developing a food allergy. However, if there are allergies to foods such as peanuts, shellfish, wheat, strawberries, citrus fruits, kiwi fruit, nuts, seeds, tomatoes, fish, eggs, or dairy products in your family, it's a good idea to be cautious when introducing solids. Breast-feeding for as long as possible will also help, especially while new foods are being introduced. Allowing a few days' gap between foods you are concerned about will allow you to spot any reaction. If in doubt, speak to your pediatrician or, if your baby is already under the care of a dietitian, ask him or her for advice.

Not all reactions to food are caused by an allergy—some are the result of a temporary food intolerance. Many children who have reactions to foods as babies can tolerate those foods by the age of three. So even if your baby does react badly to a food, he may not need to avoid it forever.

Some babies develop a rash around their mouth when they eat citrus fruits or strawberries. This is most likely to be simply a reaction to the high acid content of these foods but it could be an allergic reaction. If you are unsure, seek medical advice, and trust your baby if he refuses a food—some parents recall that, as babies, their children avoided foods that they later turned out to be allergic to.

"Oscar tried a strawberry when he was about eight months old and he got a weird rash on his face. After that, he wouldn't eat them. He squeezes them, squishes them, but he won't eat them."

Natalie, mother of Oscar, 14 months

WHEAT AND GLUTEN

There's a great deal of debate about when to introduce foods containing gluten. All foods made with wheat (for example, bread, cakes, pasta) contain gluten; some people who are gluten-intolerant cannot eat foods containing oats, barley, or rye, either, but wheat is the main culprit. Some evidence suggests that early exposure to gluten reduces the chances of intolerance, while other research suggests it should be left until after the age of one. If you have a family history of wheat intolerance or allergy it's probably a good idea to talk to your doctor before giving your baby wheat.

Luckily, it's not too difficult to avoid wheat if you want to. Most supermarkets now stock a wide range of wheat-free breads, pastas, and other products, while rice, corn, buckwheat, and quinoa are all useful alternatives in savory dishes. Flour made from older varieties of wheat, such as spelt wheat and kamut, or from sprouted wheat (as opposed to wheat grains), is often better tolerated than that made from other varieties. Ground nuts can be used as flour substitutes in some recipes (provided your child's pediatrician is not concerned about nut allergies), as can flours made from legumes, such as chickpea flour.

As far as possible, try to make sure your baby has a truly varied diet, with no single food eaten in large quantities on a daily basis. Think about whether you have developed routines that could lead to him having the same limited range of foods every day. For example, many people have dairy foods and wheat at least twice a day, every day; both are common causes of intolerance and allergy.

BLW STORY

Fern didn't even realize what food was at six months. At seven months, she started to realize that we were eating, but if we put something from our plates in front of her she didn't take much notice. It's only recently that she's trying to get at the food. And at 10 months, there's really no point in giving her purée on a spoon, it's easier to give her real food and let her work it out for herself.

She'll gnaw on a chicken bone, and if she has a chunk of banana she'll gum it a bit and spit it out and play with it, but she won't necessarily eat it. But at least she's putting it in her mouth, whereas until recently, she'd spit it out almost immediately.

We've got a lot of allergies in our family and Fern has had very bad reactions to foods that I've eaten, through my breast milk. We worked out it was grapes and pork and since I've eliminated them she's got much better. So, I'm trying to introduce the basic foods, just to see how she manages; she's only had banana, avocado, chicken, plantain, and potato. I think being slow to start on solids could be connected to her allergies.

In our family there's another baby, who's only two weeks older than Fern. She started solids at four months and has been on three meals a day for ages, so sometimes there's a bit of comparison between them. Everyone can see that Fern is doing just as well health-wise as the other baby. But they keep asking, "Is she eating yet?" Some of the family are okay with it, but some think I should start force-feeding her. I suppose they think she should be eating what everyone else eats by now. But I think, "When they're ready, they're ready." And it's not like she's wasting away, she's a big baby.

Sandra, mother of Reuben, 3, and Fern, 10 months

Whether or not you decide to avoid certain foods shouldn't affect your decision to let your baby feed himself, so long as you are careful about what you offer him. Many parents simply adapt their own meals until their baby is around a year old, leaving out the foods they don't want him to have.

Fat

Babies and young children need proportionately more fat in their diet than adults because they burn up energy easily. So if, as a family, you generally have a low-fat diet you'll need to make sure you offer your baby some foods that contain plenty of fat. There's no rush though—for the first few months of solid foods your baby should still be getting most of his nourishment from breast milk or formula, both of which contain plenty of fat.

The healthiest fats for all the family are nondairy/animal fats such as vegetable oils, oily fish, olive oil, and the oils contained in nuts and seeds. But dairy foods, such as cheese and yogurt, are good for babies; unlike adults they need the full-fat versions (not low-fat or skim).

Hydrogenated fats (or trans-fatty acids) are used in many commercially prepared foods such as cookies, cakes, pies, ready meals, and margarines and are thought to interfere with the beneficial actions of healthy fats. Foods such as these are best avoided if possible.

Fiber

Most dietary fiber is good for babies, as it helps to keep their bowels healthy. However, babies shouldn't be given raw bran or high-fiber cereals (see page 100). It's also a good idea to limit the amount of whole grains (whole-wheat bread, brown rice, whole-wheat pasta) a baby has. This is because the amount of fiber in these foods makes them very filling, meaning he may have no room left for foods with other important nutrients.

However, there's no need to switch to white bread if you normally eat whole-wheat bread, or to abandon brown rice altogether. In fact, it's probably a good idea to get your baby used to wholegrain foods early on, so that he gets a taste for them, since they tend to be more nutritious than processed foods. You simply need to make sure that he has plenty of other healthy foods to choose from so he can decide how much of the wholegrain foods to eat. Some parents alternate brown and white rice, pasta and bread so that their baby is offered a variety. (See page 194 for more information on fiber.)

Adapting Food in the Early Months

Here are some suggestions to help you adapt common foods so that your baby can eat them, too.

Fruit and vegetables

Vegetables that are hard when raw should be cut into a stick or finger shape (rather than round slices) and cooked (without salt) so that they are soft but not soggy ("al dente" may be fine for you but remember that your baby doesn't have much in the way of teeth!) Boiling or steaming is good, but a tasty alternative is to roast sticks of vegetables in the oven. This gives them a slightly crisp coating and makes them easier to grip (bear in mind that some vegetables, such as carrots, sweet potatoes and parsnips, shrink when roasted, so cut extra-wide finger shapes). Sticks of softer vegetables, such as cucumber, can be offered raw.

"The first time I gave Callum fingers of carrot they weren't steamed enough so he just sucked on them, and they got smoother and smoother. It took me a while to realize he just needed them to be steamed for a few minutes more than ours so he could actually munch them."

Ruth, mother of Callum, 18 months

Large fruits such as melon and papaya can be cut into stick shapes or wedges, while smaller ones (such as grapes) should be cut in half lengthwise, so that they are easier to handle and move around the mouth safely. Fruits such as apples, pears, and nectarines can be offered whole. Softer apples are better than firm ones as they are easier to gnaw and less likely to snap into large pieces.

It's best to leave some of the skin on most fruit and vegetables to make them easier to hold—at least until your baby is able to bite pieces off. Apples, pears, avocados, mangos and potatoes all work well with some skin left on. Your baby will soon work out how to hold the skin and scrape the flesh with his teeth (or gnaw it with his gums).

Many parents offer bananas with some skin on too: wash the skin first (in case it gets chewed), then trim it so there is an inch or so of banana sticking out and it looks like an ice-cream cone. Once your baby is more skilled, let him try the banana skinless, to work out how much pressure he can use before he squishes it completely!

Tips

- Crinkle-cutters (the gadgets that were popular in the 1970s for cutting french fries with little ridges) can be useful for cutting fruit and vegetables to make them easier for a baby to hold.

- Taking a bite out of a whole fruit before you give it to your baby will make it easier for him to get to the flesh.
- It can be handy to keep some extra portions of vegetables ready prepared in the freezer, just in case you decide to eat something that you don't want your baby to share.
- Mashed vegetables make a good not-too-runny sauce to serve with pasta.

Meat

To start with, it's best to offer meat as large pieces that can be held easily and sucked or chewed. Chicken is probably the easiest to manage at first, especially when it's given on a bone, for gnawing. Leg bones are best because they're easy to hold, and the meat on them is less crumbly than breast meat. Be sure to remove any thin splint bones first, and in general remove any gristle before offering meat to your baby.

Meat can be made more tender by stewing rather than roasting. There is no need to give large pieces every time, though—you'll soon find that your baby can manage ground meat surprisingly well with his fingers. (Ironically, it's "bite-sized" pieces that will probably be hardest for him to deal with at first, because he won't be able to get at them once he's closed his hand around them.)

Tip

You can make meat such as pork, beef, and lamb easier for your baby to chew by cutting it *across* rather than along the fibers. However, for poultry (chicken, turkey, duck, etc.), it's best to divide the meat *along* the fibers, otherwise it tends to be too crumbly to hold.

PRE-CHEWING

It's traditional in many cultures to pre-chew food for babies, to soften it and mix it with saliva so that it is easier to digest. The food is then either passed directly from the mother's mouth to the baby's as a sort of kiss or is offered to the baby by hand. Pre-chewing is most often done with meat, to break down the fibers so that the baby can manage it more easily. There is no reason why BLW parents shouldn't do this but it doesn't seem to be really necessary. Although young babies can't easily chew meat (especially red meat), they probably get a lot of goodness from just sucking it. In particular, sucking provides them with the meat juices (blood), which are rich in iron. If someone else chews the meat first, the baby may get more of the meat protein but he could lose out on some of the iron.

EASY FIRST FINGER FOODS FOR BABIES

- steamed (or lightly boiled) whole vegetables, such as green beans, baby corn, and sugar-snap peas
- steamed (or lightly boiled) florets of cauliflower and broccoli
- steamed, roasted or stir-fried vegetable sticks, such as carrot, potato, egg plant, sweet potato, parsnip, pumpkin, and zucchini
- raw sticks of cucumber (tip: keep some of these ready prepared in the fridge for babies who are teething—the coolness is soothing for their gums)

(continued on next page)

- thick slices of avocado (not too ripe or it will be very squishy)
- chicken (as a strip of meat or on a leg bone)—warm (i.e., freshly cooked) or cold
- thin strips of beef, lamb or pork—warm (i.e., freshly cooked) or cold
- fruit, such as pear, apple, banana, peach, nectarine, mango—either whole or as sticks
- sticks of firm cheese, such as cheddar or Gloucester
- breadsticks
- rice cakes or toast "fingers"—on their own or with a homemade spread, such as hummus and tomato, or cottage cheese

And, if you want to be a bit more adventurous, try making your own versions of:

- meatballs or mini-burgers
- lamb or chicken nuggets
- fishcakes or fish fingers
- falafels
- lentil patties
- rice balls (made with sushi rice, or basmati rice with dhal)

Remember, you don't need to use recipes specifically designed for babies, provided you're careful to keep salt and sugar to a minimum.

Bread

Bread can be a good finger food, but babies under a year old shouldn't have more than two slices a day because it tends to be high in salt. Most breads are easier for young babies to cope with if they are toasted than if they are soft. White bread, in particular, goes quite doughy once it's wet and can be difficult to manage in the mouth—especially when it's very fresh. Flat breads, such as chapattis, pita, and naan, are less crumbly, so may be easier for your baby to handle at first.

Breadsticks are handy for dipping into soft foods such as hummus; they can be given to your baby ready loaded until he is able to "dip" for himself. Salt-free rice cakes are a good alternative to bread, particularly for spreading with soft food or a thick sauce.

Pasta

Pasta twists (fusilli), shells, and bows are less slippery and easier to grip than smoother shapes; your baby will probably find most foods—including pasta—easier to manage "dry" (i.e., without any sauce) at first. Try offering some with sauce and some without so he can try both.

> "At the beginning I was doing lots of steamed vegetables and cutting them into finger shapes for Matthew, and we would eat something different. Matthew didn't seem to mind, he was quite happy with his plate of vegetables. Now, whatever we're eating, we offer him some, although I still do some separate things. My husband says that I cook for Matthew in a way that I've never cooked for him. I've been making Matthew little

meatballs and homemade fish fingers, and homemade pizzas, and trying to give him quite a lot of fish, too."

Carly, mother of Matthew, 14 months

"To start with we gave Maria pieces of well-steamed carrot, bits of pear or apple, or chunks of chicken or lamb; whatever was for dinner. She had broccoli quite early, which she loved. She'd just suck on it like a lollipop—now she's chewing the top off and getting a lot down."

Alison, mother of Maria, 7 months

Rice

Rice is a good, nutritious base for a meal but parents some-times find they need to adapt the way they cook it or the type of rice they use to make it easier for their baby to manage.

Short-grain rices such as Thai rice, Japanese sushi rice, or risotto rice (or even pudding rice) are naturally sticky and easy to grab in handfuls; ordinary long-grain rice is less sticky but is easier for babies to handle if it's either slightly overcooked or cooked the day before it's eaten (but see page 224 for important safety information about storing rice).

However, all babies will eventually find a way of dealing with ordinary boiled rice: some simply put their faces quite close to the plate and "shovel" the rice in; others enjoy practic-ing their pincer grip (using thumb and forefinger to pick things up) by selecting one grain at a time—it's a bit slow, but a lot of fun (and very good for hand-eye coordination).

Will, 5 months, is using his mouth to find out about everyday objects; he'll do the same thing in a few weeks with his first solid foods ▷

For Jack, at 6 months, this banana is a completely new thing to be examined — first by touch, sight and smell, and then by taste ▾

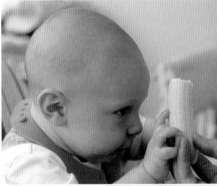

These vegetables are just the right size and shape for 6-month-old babies like Lilly to manage ▷

◁ Babies are curious about food —Tessa (just over 6 months) is fascinated by these carrot sticks

◀ Felix (6 months) is using both hands to guide his cheese on toast to his mouth, but he hasn't yet learnt which end to hold

Six-month-old George has his eye on some of his big sister's carrots ▼

Owen, 6½ months, is working out how to keep hold of a slippery chunk of beetroot from his mum's salad ▼

At 7 months, Lara finds it helpful to use her fingers to keep foods like melon in her mouth while she chews ▼

Charlie, not yet 7 months, is already used to sharing family meals and is able to pick out a piece of meat from this casserole ▶

Max (7 months) is holding his broccoli by the stalk so that he can munch the top ▼

▲ Eating out is easy with baby-led weaning; George (7 months) decides what to go for from his mum's plate

◀ Aidan, at 7½ months, is discovering how noodles work

Jamie (7 months) and his granddad enjoy a pub lunch together now and then ▶

Oscar (8 months) has worked out how to separate the flesh of his pineapple from the skin ▼

◀ Eight-month-old Robert is holding his strawberry carefully, so that he can take small bites from it

Hannah (8 months) wants to try having her falafels in pitta bread – just like her dad

At 8½ months William can happily manage a lunchtime avocado sandwich

Although Seren (9 months) has only two teeth she is having no trouble eating her apple ▸

◀ Lila (9 months) has learnt to pick up small pieces of minced meat with her thumb and forefinger; she then concentrates while she puts them into her mouth ▼

◀ At 10 months, Oscar uses his hand *and* his spoon to eat his porridge

Aidan (10 months) won't eat the whole of this lamb chop, but he will get a lot of goodness from gnawing and sucking on it ▶

◄ Babies often choose unusual combinations of food. Orban, 9 months, is eating a plum with his toast

At 10 months, Orban shows that fingers are the perfect 'dipper' for soft foods such as hummus ▼

Nisha (10 months) enjoys lots of different foods; today she has decided to start her lunch with a strawberry ▼

Max (1 year) and his dad are enjoying sharing some chicken ▶

Charlie, 1 year, shares Sunday lunch with her family and is getting to grips with cutlery ▼

Madeleine (15 months) is concentrating hard to use a picnic fork to eat pasta salad ▼

◀ By serving himself, Owen (17 months) is learning to judge volume and distance as well as how to gauge his own appetite

Dips and Dippers

Most babies can dip from about nine months, but as with everything, some will be able to do it much earlier (or later) than others. Using a "dipper" can be a lot of fun. It means your baby can eat soft or runny foods such as yogurt without a spoon, and it's also a good way for him to acquire the skills needed for using a spoon later. He may discover dipping for himself with any piece of food that works—be ready for some odd combinations, such as using a finger of roasted sweet potato to dip into pudding!

Ideas for dippers

- breadsticks
- pieces of chapatti, pita bread, or toast
- oat cakes or rice cakes (salt-free)—these may be easier to dip if they are broken in half first
- sticks of firm fruit, such as apple
- raw vegetable sticks: carrot, celery (strings removed), red or green peppers, zucchini, cucumber, green beans, sugar-snap peas
- lightly steamed whole baby corn
- roasted vegetable fingers: carrots, pumpkin and other squashes, parsnip, zucchini, potatoes, sweet potatoes, etc.

Easy-to-make savory dips

Many of the following dips can be bought ready-made, but most are very easy and quick to make at home. They usually have a couple of basic ingredients that are blended with olive oil or yogurt in a food processor.

- hummus
- guacamole
- mixed bean dip
- kidney bean and tomato
- red pepper and butter bean
- cheese sauce dip
- cream cheese and yogurt with chives
- yogurt and tofu
- yogurt and cucumber
- dhal (lentils with spices)
- eggplant dip (baba ganoush)

Breakfast

Parents new to BLW often wonder what they can give their baby for breakfast. They find it hard to imagine him eating the same foods as they do in the morning. However, there's every chance your baby won't be at all interested in breakfast to start with—at that time of day many babies just want to snuggle up and have a milk feeding. Once he does start to take an interest the following tips and ideas may be useful:

- Babies can often manage mushy things such as cereal and milk fairly well with their fingers if they're allowed to practice, so he may be able to share what everyone else is eating.
- Remember to allow plenty of time—breakfast can be very rushed in many households, and babies need time both to experiment with food and to eat.
- Offer your baby plenty of variety throughout the week (many adults get into the habit of having the same breakfast every day).

BLW STORY

It took two or three months for me to feel confident about trusting that Benjamin would eat what he needs. You hear people saying, "They've got to have iron after six months ... they've got to have this and they've got to have that," and so I used to worry whether he was getting enough goodness. For example, I thought it'd be good for him to have lentils, but I didn't know how to get them into him. (I totally forgot that you could put them on toast or rice cakes.)

So I panicked a bit and thought: "If I do purées as well as BLW, at least I can be sure that he's getting some nutrition from the foods that he can't easily pick up and chew." I did puréeing for a couple of months, but it took about two hours' work every night just to do all his food for the following day. When he was about 10 months he started eating a bit more, and we went back to just doing BLW. I wish I hadn't lost faith, really, because it would have been a lot easier if I'd just kept going.

And, of course, we discovered that Benjamin liked being in control of what he was eating; he far preferred feeding himself to being spoon-fed. He became very suspicious about what was on the spoon. If we managed to get a little bit in, maybe he'd decide to eat it, but, really, we were just shoving a spoon in his mouth to see whether he liked what was on it—and sometimes he did, but sometimes he didn't. It just felt like a big responsibility getting nutrition into him at first.

Jana, mother of Benjamin, 13 months

- Read labels carefully: many commercial brands of cereals (especially those aimed at children) have very high levels of sugar and salt.
- Cereals coated in chocolate, honey, or sugar should be avoided altogether, along with high-fiber bran-based cereals (see pages 100 and 105 for more on fiber).

BREAKFAST IDEAS

- Fresh fruit.
- Hot cereal. While cooking you can add: stewed or grated apples or pears, blackberries or blueberries, dried apricots, dates, cranberries or figs. Fruit purée, strawberries, or a little molasses can be added at the table. Although hot cereal is usually made from oatmeal, it can also be made with rice flakes, millet flakes, and quinoa flakes (usually available in health food shops but more and more super-markets are stocking them).
- Live, full-fat natural yogurt with fresh fruit. (Babies and toddlers often love stirring berries or stewed or puréed fruit into their yogurt, or dipping pieces of fruit into it.)
- Scrambled egg (well cooked).
- Cold cereal—with or without milk. Some babies love dry cereal; others prefer it mushy. Cereals such as mini wheats, cornflakes and Rice Krispies are suitable for babies because they don't have high levels of sugar and salt.
- Toast, oat cakes, or rice cakes spread with cream cheese or 100 percent fruit spread.
- Baked beans on toast.
- Cheese on toast

Easy Snacks and Food on the Move

Once your baby starts to rely on solid foods to fill his tummy it's a good idea to make sure you have a healthy snack with you when you go out together, just in case he gets hungry before you get home. The following are a few ideas for foods that are easy to carry with you:

- fruit (such as apples, pears, and bananas)
- salad (tomatoes, sticks of cucumber, peppers, and celery with strings removed)
- cold cooked vegetables (carrots, broccoli, etc.)
- cold cooked corn-on-the-cob
- sandwiches
- pieces of cheese
- pasta salad (or cold cooked pasta)
- yogurt—plain, full-fat, live yogurt with fresh fruit added is best (flavored yogurts often contain a lot of sugar)
- avocado dip or hummus, with breadsticks, carrot sticks, etc.
- low-salt oat cakes, rice cakes, or toast, spread with cream cheese or sugar-free fruit spreads
- dried apricots or other dried fruits (in moderation—they can damage teeth if given too often). Brands that have not been treated with sulfur dioxide are best. (Nonsulfured apricots are usually dark brown, rather than bright orange)
- freshly made fruit smoothies
- dry, low-sugar breakfast cereal

Remember to read labels very carefully. Teething biscuits and many prepackaged snacks aimed at children tend to be full of sugar and additives and are best avoided.

Desserts

There are plenty of nutritious desserts you can offer your baby and an occasional sweet dish won't do him any harm. But having dessert with every meal (even if it's just a sweetened yogurt) will encourage him to develop a "sweet tooth" and may mean he begins to expect a sweet food every time. His taste buds are being programmed during these formative first years of eating and you can help him to develop good (or bad) eating habits that will last a lifetime. Having a dessert at every meal can also make it all too easy to slip into a "finish your vegetables and then you can have dessert" scenario, especially if your baby likes to take his time over his main course.

If you do want to have a dessert, go for a healthy (preferably homemade) one wherever possible. Even commercially made "healthy options" often have high levels of artificial sweeteners and additives. Bear in mind that if everyone else is eating something, your baby will want to try it, too—so if you don't want him eating an unhealthy dessert, either have it when he's gone to bed, or see if you can offer him something that looks almost identical (this doesn't always work!). However, if you can make your dessert as nutritious as your main course then you won't have to worry too much if, occasionally, your baby eats only the sweet dish.

. . . .
HEALTHY DESSERTS

- fresh fruit
- fruit salad
- plain full-fat live yogurt with fresh or stewed fruit
- homemade rice pudding
- homemade egg custard
- apple crumble (made with sweet eating apples rather than cooking apples so you don't need to add much sugar)
- baked pears or apples
. . . .

"We don't tend to eat too many sweet things at home but if I'm out for a meal and I have dessert, then Mila will share it. I don't believe in not letting her have things that I'm having, because it seems hypocritical. Of course, I probably shouldn't be having it either, really! But I'm not going to say, 'Oh no, that's just for grownups,' because it's not fair—and it makes the sweet thing much more desirable to her."   *Carmen, mother of Mila, 2*

Q&A

Don't babies have to start with one taste at a time?

Parents used to be told (and still are, sometimes) that it's important to start with one new taste and stick with it for a few days, to make sure that their baby doesn't react badly to it, before adding another new food. Unless you have food allergies in your family (see page 102), there is no need to follow this advice if you are doing BLW. There are two reasons for this: first, the digestive system of a six-month-old baby is a lot more mature than that of a baby of four months (when solids used to be introduced), so digestive problems are unlikely, and second, a baby who is allowed to feed himself with solid foods will naturally eat only very small amounts at first, and may well try just one or two new foods at a time anyway.

One of the most important aspects of BLW is the chance for babies to taste food before they eat it. If they are offered a few different foods at once, they can choose which one they want to concentrate on—coming back to the others later, or on another day. This may have positive implications for the baby's health: some parents who have followed BLW have found that a food that their baby didn't seem to want in the beginning turned out later to be something he was allergic to. If instinctively avoiding a potential allergen really *is* something that babies can do, then it is obviously easier for them to do it if they are given foods that they can separate easily. So it makes sense to let them experiment with, for example, a "meat-and-two-veg" dinner or a fruit salad, presented in the same form as for the rest of the family, rather than for them to be given the same food as a single mixture, puréed, or mashed up together. This is an aspect of BLW that may make it a particularly useful approach for families with allergies.

Are mesh feeders an appropriate way to begin BLW?

Mesh feeders are promoted as a way of allowing babies to munch on "real" foods without the risk of choking, but they aren't necessary—and they don't fit with what BLW is about. A mesh feeder may work for a baby who isn't old enough to be able to sit upright, or hold onto a piece of food and get it to his mouth accurately without losing his grip, but that baby shouldn't really be having solid foods yet. If he isn't mature enough to feed himself without the need for a gadget like this, then he probably isn't really ready to digest solid foods either.

Once your baby can sit up and reach for food, he wants to be able to see it and examine its shape and texture, not just taste it. He can't do that if it's inside a piece of plastic netting. Remember that, for your baby, the first solid foods are about exploration and discovery, not eating. A mesh feeder may be an exciting new toy that happens to have a taste, but it won't help him learn what real food looks and feels like—nor will it help him learn how to manage food in his mouth. Provided the baby is sitting upright and is in control of his eating (see pages 91–92) choking is no more of a risk with BLW that with any other method of weaning. All in all, for a baby who is ready to explore solids, using a mesh feeder is an unnecessary distraction that may prevent him from learning about and enjoying his food.

Does my baby need vitamin supplements?

Research has shown that breast milk or formula alone fulfills a baby's nutrient needs for the first six months and, in theory, babies ought to be able to get any extra nutrients they need from solid foods after this age. However, to be on the safe side, some pediatricians will recommend supplements of vitamins A, C, and D for babies who are breast-fed beyond six months, and in some instances, for formula-fed babies who are drinking less than 500 ml of formula per day. If you are considering starting vitamin supplements, be sure to check with your pediatrician first. Supplements are generally given in liquid form, as drops.

Giving babies vitamin supplements can help to provide a nutritional "cushion" for families that don't eat a particularly good diet, or don't have access to nutritious food. It may also compensate for modern food production and storage methods that mean much of the food we buy has already lost some of its nutrients by the time it reaches us.

Certain groups of babies (and their mothers) may be short on vitamin D. Most of our vitamin D comes from the action of sunlight on our skin, but in many areas of the globe the sunlight in the winter months isn't strong enough to make vitamin D. Things are worse for people with dark skin, which tends not to absorb sunlight well. Too-frequent use of sunblock can also prevent the skin from making enough vitamin D. Most at risk are women who cover their face and body or rarely go outside. Vitamin D supplements are recommended for pregnant and breast-feeding mothers in these groups, as well as for their babies.

In general, however, it is worth bearing in mind that fussy eaters are more at risk of not getting enough vitamins and minerals than children who enjoy a wide range of foods. The experience of parents who have tried BLW is overwhelmingly that babies who are allowed to be in charge of their own weaning and to make choices over what foods to eat are much less likely to be fussy eaters than those who have these decisions made for them. This suggests that BLW is in itself a good way to help ensure that your baby has a balanced diet with plenty of nutrients.

It's best to focus on making sure that you offer your baby the foods that contain the necessary vitamins and minerals in the first place (see pages 198–199). Eating foods when they are as fresh as possible, and using cooking and storage methods that help to conserve nutrients can also help (see page 185).

I've heard that cows' milk is important for babies but also that it is linked to asthma and eczema. Which is right?

All mammal milks are designed to provide the baby animal of that species with all the nutrients he needs, in the right proportions. The only milk which can do this for human babies is human breast milk. If young children drink too much cows' milk it can dull their appetite so that they don't eat enough other foods, possibly making them anemic, or otherwise undernourished. This is why cows' milk is not recommended as a drink for babies under a year old.

There are substantial numbers of people who are allergic to cows' milk and it's one of the things best left out of your baby's diet if you have a strong family history of allergies. (Goats' and sheep's milk are alternatives to cows' milk but they are equally likely to trigger an allergy.)

Having said all that, cows' milk is a good source of protein, calcium, fat, and vitamins A, B, and D, and it's cheap and plentiful—which is why it is added to so many other foods. In fact, unless you are really vigilant, it's hard never to give your child cows' milk in some form. It is also an easy food to cook with, and is the basis of many puddings and sauces. So it can be a very useful part of the developing diet for many babies. But it shouldn't assume more importance than any other single food.

If you want to include cows' milk in your child's diet:

- Treat milk as a food rather than a drink. Use it in cooking or, once your child is over a year, offer a small amount as part of a snack (perhaps with some bread and fruit), allowing him to choose whether to drink or reject it.
- Start offering him full-fat dairy foods such as cheese, butter, and yogurt any time after six months.

If you would prefer to avoid dairy products altogether:

- Make sure your baby gets plenty of protein, calcium, vitamins A, B, and D and fat from his other foods (see Chapter 7).
- You may wish to try alternatives to animal milk, such as "milks" made from rice, oats and soy. These are not milks in the true sense but can be used in similar ways in some recipes. (However they, too, can trigger allergies.)
- It may be a good idea to consult a nutritionist or dietitian, just to make sure you're providing your baby with a balanced diet. This is particularly important if you are avoiding a range of foods because of concerns about allergies.

My mom keeps asking me if my son has had cereal yet. Why is cereal so important? He seems happy trying out vegetables and fruit for now. He's nearly seven months.

Rice cereal has traditionally been a baby's first solid food since the 1950s, usually given by spoon from three or four months onward. This emphasis on cereal seems to have been partly because it's a bland food, so it was thought that babies would accept it readily and digest it easily, and partly because of the belief that babies needed calories to "build them up" and make them healthy. Modern cereals marketed for babies are usually fortified with iron—but the small amounts of iron that babies need can be found easily in other foods (see answer to next question, below).

We now know that cereals aren't necessary as a first food because:

- most babies under six months don't need anything other than milk
- babies and young children need a balanced diet, not one which contains too much carbohydrate

Cereals are high in starch. This means they are digested very slowly and are very filling, so giving a young baby even a little cereal can spoil his appetite for his milk feedings. Breast milk (or formula) is far too important to babies' health to be replaced by less-nutritious foods that they don't need. But giving babies foods that are filling is still seen by some people as a good thing, often because they believe it will make their little one sleep for longer.

However, provided they are not introduced before six months, cereals shouldn't interfere with your baby's overall nourishment—as long as *he* is the one who decides how much of them to eat. The problem is that cereals lend themselves to spoon-feeding—which makes it very easy to give more than just a taste.

When babies of six months are first starting solids the most important thing is to offer them foods they can handle and munch easily. Cooked vegetables and raw or cooked fruit are ideal for this. They are also tasty, colorful, and full of important vitamins and minerals—without being too filling. Offering some meat occasionally is a good idea because of the iron and zinc content, but there's really not much need for starchy foods at this stage.

So it's fine to offer cereals to your baby as part of a range of foods—perhaps in the form of bread or as fistfuls of rice to pick up—but they don't have to be the first food. Above all, remember that offering your baby a variety of foods and allowing him to choose what to eat, and how much, will give him the best chance of getting all the nutrients he needs, in the right proportions.

My baby is eight months old and still eats very little. He seems happy enough and he's growing and developing well, but I've been told we should be "making sure" he has plenty of iron, especially as he's breast-fed. How can we do this with BLW?

It's true that breast milk doesn't contain as much iron as, for example, meat or fortified foods. But the iron in breast milk is absorbed extremely easily. (Formula contains a lot of iron but it is not easily absorbed.)

As well as the iron they get from breast milk babies also have reserves that were built up while they were in the womb. These gradually get used up, so that some time after six months, they begin to need more iron than they can get from breast milk alone. But the difference isn't huge—breast milk can still provide most of what they need. So your baby is probably getting enough from the small amount of food he is eating.

The most important thing is that your baby should have a variety of foods to choose from, as this will give him the best chance to eat what he needs. Meat and meat products are an excellent source of iron. And both meat and foods that contain vitamin C help the stomach to absorb iron from plant sources when eaten at the same meal. Many foods (for example breakfast cereals and many breads) are fortified with iron. By providing your baby with the opportunity to eat meat, together with a range of fruits and vegetables and some iron-fortified foods, you will be helping him to get as much iron as possible from his diet.

Try offering meat in different forms (including ground) to give your baby the best chance of getting it to his mouth and eating it. Remember, though, that much of the iron in meat is in the juices (blood), so that sucking a slice or chunk will provide him with goodness even though he may not be able to chew it properly yet.

Good sources of iron for vegetarians include eggs; legumes, such as beans, lentils and peas; dried fruits such as apricots, figs, and prunes; and green leafy vegetables. It's particularly important for vegetarians to have foods that are rich in vitamin C with their meals to help with iron absorption. (See Chapter 7 for more details.)

Is it all right to give my baby deli meat? Are certain kinds better than others? What about hot dogs?

Pregnant women are often advised to avoid deli meats because of the risk of infection for their unborn baby, but this precaution isn't necessary when babies are moving on to solid foods. However, most deli meats, such as salami, are processed, which means that nutrients are lost and—usually—chemicals are added. These can include flavors and colors, ingredients to give the food a long shelf life, and "fillers," such as potato starch, that allow the meat to be sold more cheaply. Processed foods tend to contain high levels of salt, too.

Babies, even more than adults, need to have food that is as nutritious as possible. This is partly because their brains and bodies are still growing and developing (so they need the very best building blocks) and partly because their stomachs cannot sift through large quantities of food in order to extract just a few key nutrients.

In general, the more highly processed the food, the worse it is for babies. So a hot dog will provide less nutrition (and more potentially harmful chemicals and salt) than a slice of ham cooked on the bone. Go for organic "real" meat whenever you can.

If you do purchase deli meats, buy only those that have been stored at the correct temperature (away from raw meats)—and take similar care when storing them at home (see page 223 for more on food safety).

5.

After the Early Days

"It's been fascinating to watch her deal with so many different types of food and see her skills developing. One week she can't manage a handful of rice, and maybe the next week she can, and then you notice that she's able to pick up a few grains of rice between her fingers. And then nothing happens for ages and suddenly she's able to actually pick up a spoon and put it in her own mouth. But we can't teach her anything—we just have to sit back and watch her learn."

Margaret, mother of Esther, 21 months

Progressing at Your Baby's Pace

As your baby progresses with solid food you'll see her skills develop as she learns to handle a wide range of flavors, textures, and shapes. However, many parents find that their baby's progress isn't as smooth as they expect. Some babies make an enthusiastic start but then become less interested in food for a week or two; many take a while before they actually eat very much at all. All of this is normal with BLW. Expectations about how quickly babies should increase their food intake are often unrealistic and based on a method of weaning in which the parent—not the baby—is in charge. It seems that, when they are allowed to make their own decisions, very few naturally choose to follow a set pattern. So it's best not to think too much about what "should" happen and just let your baby set the pace.

If you include your baby in all your own meals and let her decide how many milk feedings she wants she'll naturally move toward eating three main meals (and, later, as many snacks as she needs) in her own time. But it may not happen as soon as you expect. Parents are sometimes told that all babies should be on three meals a day by eight months but although most babies may be keen to handle and play with food three times a day at this age, many still won't be eating much, and even more won't want anything other than breast milk or formula for breakfast. There's no point in trying to rush your baby—it won't make her learn any faster, and she'll probably get upset and frustrated. It's much better to keep mealtimes enjoyable and let her decide when she's ready to eat more.

It's also fairly common for babies to go through a "lull" at some point between seven and nine months, when progress with solids seems nonexistent and their weight gain slows down a little. As long as your baby is well, is having plenty of milk feedings, and is included in your mealtimes, this isn't anything to worry about. It's usually short-lived and is often followed by a sudden increase in both appetite and feeding skills. Many parents describe this as when their baby "suddenly got it," and started to "really" eat.

Whether or not you experience a lull, at some point you'll probably notice your baby playing less with her food and eating more purposefully. Starting to "really" eat like this can happen any time from eight or nine months to around a year, and often (but not always) coincides with the baby gradually asking for less milk; the best approach is to let your baby's appetite and abilities guide you. Keep offering her plenty of opportunities to practice her new skills on a variety of foods, and someone (you!) to copy, and let her take her time. You'll probably find that by around nine or ten months she is eating pretty much the same range of foods as the rest of the family and that you don't need to think too hard about how to prepare her food because she can manage most things without a problem.

> "When Jake was about a year old I realized that he was actually starting to eat for eating's sake, rather than just getting to know food. There was a definite shift, away from play and into eating—as though he needed to fill his belly."
>
> Vicky, mother of Jake, 3

Adventurous Taste Buds

Once you and your baby have made a start with BLW, it's a good idea to make sure she experiences a really wide range of flavors. The more variety she has now, the more readily she'll try new things when she's older. Many parents automatically give their baby plain food such as steamed vegetables or fruit for the first few weeks of solid foods, but there's no need to restrict her to the bland flavors that are associated with commercial baby foods.

All babies are exposed to different tastes in the womb because they swallow amniotic fluid that contains traces of the flavors of foods the mother has eaten. Breast-fed babies get different-tasting milk too, according to their mother's diet. They usually enjoy new flavors, even quite strong ones, especially if their mother eats them often. In fact, studies suggest that breast-fed babies are programmed to accept flavors that are familiar to them from breast milk (for example, garlic), possibly because this is a way of showing them that these foods are safe. And yet many people believe that a baby's first solid foods need to be almost tasteless. Indeed, in some cultures there is a belief that young children won't eat vegetables and meat—and as a result they tend to be restricted to cereals, such as rice, until they are as old as two years. This is not only unnecessary but is probably boring for the child—and may lead to undernutrition.

Using herbs, spices, and highly flavored vegetables in your cooking is not only good for taste but may be good for the family's health, too, since many of these foods have their own health-giving properties and nutrients. A wide variety of healthy foods and flavors is also more likely to give your baby a good range of vitamins and minerals.

Babies who feed themselves are more likely to try new foods and be adventurous with flavors than babies who are fed by someone else, because eating is enjoyable for them. The following tips are good to bear in mind:

- Always let your baby decide if she wants to eat some-thing—there's no need to persuade her if she doesn't seem to want it.
- Your baby will taste new foods at the front of her mouth and spit them out if she doesn't like them—it's important not to try to prevent her from doing this. Being allowed to reject anything she doesn't like helps to ensure that she learns to trust food. (This may be one reason why so many babies who are spoon-fed refuse new foods—purées are much harder to spit out.)

- Let your baby share mealtimes with the rest of the family so that she can copy what everyone else is eating—if you are all eating curry and enjoying it your baby's curiosity will almost certainly make her want to try it.
- Give your baby the chance to try foods that you don't normally eat as well as your regular family meals, so she is offered the maximum variety of tastes.

"We gave Isabella a really wide range of tastes right from the start—as many things as we could think of—and now she'll eat just about anything. It's great when we're traveling. She's always eaten things like sauerkraut, chili, chicken piri piri—she's got broader tastes than many adults I know."

Jennifer, mother of Isabella, 4

Some parents of babies who have been formula-fed (and whose feedings for the first six months have therefore all tasted the same) have noticed that their babies are less adventurous with flavors at first. This doesn't usually last long, though, and, in general, most are keen to experiment, even with strong flavors. However hesitant your baby is, the more opportunity she is given to try different foods and the more she is able to copy the example of others, the less cautious she is likely to be as time goes on.

Many BLW babies have surprised their parents by tasting some spicy or hot food and then going back for more. Even if there are foods that you only have now and then, or when you eat out, try to include your baby in the meal so she can taste it too. As long as it's not *too* hot, of course—don't expect her to enjoy a spicy curry just yet! (Most cultures that eat a lot of spicy foods start babies off with mild versions of the family dishes.) There's no need to persuade her if she doesn't want to taste it—some foods have very strong smells that she may need to get used to. Most spicy dishes are served with something plain, such as rice or noodles, so she won't go hungry. Have some water or plain yogurt on hand in case she does find the food too spicy—and remember to taste the food yourself first, and take out any hot chili peppers before your little one tries it.

INTRODUCING SPICY FOODS

A simple, thick dhal made from lentils can be a good way to introduce your baby to spicy food. You can add all sorts of vegetables and gradually increase the amounts of spices, or try different combinations. Lentils are nutritious, with lots of protein and iron. Pita, chapatti, or toast can be used as a dipper or the dhal can be eaten in handfuls or in balls, mixed with rice, or offered to your baby on a preloaded spoon so she can feed herself with it.

"When Harriet was about nine months old we went out for curry. She was eating rice really well by then and she grabbed a handful from my plate, and it had some curry sauce on it. The thing is, the curry was really hot—it was actually too hot for me. Before I could do anything, she had crammed it into her mouth. I was expecting her to go completely ballistic. But she just sort of thought about it, then swallowed it and reached for some more."

Jen, mother of Harriet, 2

Learning About Textures

As well as offering your baby a variety of flavors, remember that she also needs to experience different textures. Most textures—runny, crunchy, chewy, mushy, etc.—are likely to be in your meals anyway, if you eat a varied diet, so there's no need to limit your baby to foods you think she'll be able to pick up easily. Exploring a full range of textures will help her to develop important skills which are relevant to eating, the prevention of choking (see page 46), and even speech. She'll also enjoy discovering different consistencies.

Your baby will be remarkably inventive at getting foods of different textures into her mouth before she learns to use silverware. This is when you need your camera! Your baby (and everything around her) may well get covered in whatever it is she is trying to eat. She may suck at spaghetti, shovel rice or minced meat into her mouth, gnaw at chicken bones, try eating straight off the plate, lick the plate clean, or pick up peas one by one—possibly even popping them into her mouth unexpectedly fast (this is fantastic practice for hand-eye coordination). However you prepare your family's food, your baby will find a way of eating it.

Textures don't only come in "hard" and "soft"—there are lots of in-betweens and subtle differences. For example:

- Roasted vegetables have a crunchy outside but a soft inside.
- Toasted bread crusts are hard and dry, whereas apples are hard but moist.
- Pears can be hard or soft (and really juicy!), depending on how ripe they are, while vegetables can be either crisp or mushy, depending on how long you cook them.

- Foods such as wafer cookies are crunchy to bite but go soft almost as soon as they hit the tongue.
- Bananas are firm to bite, then soft to chew—while mashed potato is soft to bite *and* chew.
- Cheddar cheese is hard and can be sucked for ages. Feta cheese crumbles easily.
- Meat is springy, while white fish is soft and crumbly.
- Mashed potato can be dry and floury, soft and sticky—or almost runny.
- A chicken drumstick has both the texture of the flesh and the hardness of the bone (and working out how to separate the chicken from the bone can be challenging and fun).
- Cream cheeses are soft but sticky, so your baby will need to find out how to use her tongue to help her move them around her mouth.

CRUNCHY TEXTURES ARE FUN

There is research that suggests that we get particular enjoyment out of eating crunchy foods. It seems that massive bursts of ultrasound are generated with the very first bite and that these trigger pleasure receptors in the brain. This suggests that babies who are given only purées at first are missing out on an important source of pleasure—something that BLW babies may associate with mealtimes for years to come.

"Naresh first took some rice from my plate when he was about eight and a half months—a handful at first, and then he started picking it up grain by grain and very carefully putting each grain into his mouth. It hadn't occurred to me to offer him anything other than sticks of vegetables until then. It always takes me by surprise how well he can manage different foods."

Rashmi, mother of Naresh, 10 months

Runny Foods

Although most parents enjoy seeing how inventive their baby is with different textures they often draw the line at letting their baby feed herself with runny food. This is partly because they can't imagine how she will eat it without being spoon-fed, and partly because they dread the inevitable mess. But babies are remarkably adaptable and will quickly find their own way to manage semiliquid food such as cereal or yogurt. Some are very good at using their fingers to deal with even the runniest food; others seem to prefer *not* to lick their fingers and find, for example, that "drinking" yogurt straight from the container works best.

Many babies quickly learn how to use a "dipper" (such as a breadstick) or a spoon to dip into runny foods (see page 113), sometimes long before they understand how spoons work. Others can manage a spoon when it is given to them to hold ready-loaded, even though they aren't yet able to load it without help. Alternatively, if you make cereals or sauces a little thicker for your baby, you may find that she can get soft handfuls to her mouth, or, if it's thick enough, it can be spread on rice cakes, oat cakes, or toast. Babies find soup is easier to manage if it has lumps left in that can be fished out; if the soup is smooth or thin, bread or breadsticks can be used to dip into it, and rice or pieces of bread can be used to thicken it.

The key to success with BLW is to see things from the baby's point of view and try to forget the rules that adults apply to eating. There's no need to worry about table manners for now—they'll come eventually—your baby needs to master food in her own way first. As for the mess, well, there's nothing you can do to prevent it, but you can prepare for it so it's not too much work to clean up (see page 83). Remember that you don't have to give your child runny foods every day, and this stage of messy eating doesn't last long. You'll miss the cute baby face covered in yogurt when she's older—honestly!

Most important, never scold your baby for making a mess or let her know that it bothers you at all. It's not uncommon for babies to develop phobias, as toddlers, over foods that they associate with an unpleasant atmosphere, and it's easy to see how runny or messy foods could be a problem later if a baby's early experiences with them are stressful. It's one of the keys to successful BLW: always keep mealtimes enjoyable.

> "I made a thick split pea and ham soup, and Fay abso-
> lutely loved it. I gave her a spoon, and she dipped it in
> and sucked it a bit. But in the end she abandoned the
> spoon and just put her face in the bowl. (We used a
> suction bowl, but I had to hold the top of it so she didn't
> tip it completely upside down.) After that she put her
> hands in and seemed to get an enormous amount of
> soup. That was one of the first really successful things.
> And that was relatively early on; she was less than seven
> months when we did that."
>
> Janice, mother of Alfie, 4, and Fay, 7 months

Feast and Famine

Once your baby has been on solids for a few months you can expect to see a pattern emerging with her food intake as she learns that food can stop her feeling hungry. However, although she'll probably eat more than she did in the first months of experimenting, you may be surprised at just how much the amount she eats varies—from feast one day to famine the next. Some babies go days without apparently eating much at all, then suddenly switch to eating up everything in sight. As long as you offer her nutritious food, you simply need to trust your baby's appetite and instinct to know what she needs and when she needs it. If she is still demanding plenty of milk feedings, she is not going to go hungry.

> "I would probably describe Robert as a typical child when it comes to eating: he'll eat nothing for three days and then he'll eat lots for the next three days. I was exactly the same—apparently my mom would always say, 'I'm not worried, because I know that in x number of days, she'll eat like a horse.'"
>
> *Kath, mother of Euan, 3,*
> *and Robert, 18 months*

Your Baby's Diaper

One of the biggest changes you'll notice when your baby gets going with solids is the change in her stool. The bowel movement of a fully breast-fed baby is soft, runny and yellow, and it smells very mild (almost sweet, some parents say). For the first month or so of life breast-fed babies will fill their diaper several times a day but after about four to six weeks they can suddenly change to pooping only once every few days. Some have been known to go as long as three weeks without a bowel movement. Provided the baby is otherwise well, this is perfectly normal; it is not constipation.

Formula-fed babies have a slightly darker and more formed

stool from birth and they may fill their diapers a bit less often in the beginning. Their stool smells slightly stronger than breast-fed babies'. They can also become constipated, especially in hot weather, which is why parents are advised to offer them extra drinks of water.

When you first start offering your baby solid food she'll probably just play with it; the first sign that she has actually *swallowed* some may well be when you see "bits" in her stool (this is easier to see in the soft stool of a breast-fed baby). You may even be able to recognize the food from earlier that day or the day before (sometimes this is not at all what you'd expect: for example, banana can appear as black wormlike streaks). This doesn't mean that your baby can't digest the food; it just shows that her body is adjusting to it and developing the enzymes needed to break it down. It will also happen less as she learns to chew foods thoroughly before swallowing.

Gradually, your baby's bowel movements will become more solid and darker in color although, for a breast-fed baby who is still having lots of drinks at the breast, loose stools may still be the norm. But the most noticeable change will be the smell! This can be quite unexpected when you have gotten used to the smell from a milk-only diet, but it is perfectly normal. Your baby may pass wind slightly more often, too—or it may just be that her farts are more noticeable because they are smelly!

Some babies get a slightly sore bottom when their bowel movements start to change. If this happens, you just need to be alert and ready to change your baby's diaper the minute she has filled it.

"His poop changed quite soon; it was only about five or six weeks in. We were so proud—it was Cameron's first proper poop. He was only pooping a couple of times a week before, now it's every day. And it's never changed back—he must be eating more than we realize."

Sophie, mother of Cameron, 8 months

"Alanna started putting food in her mouth from around six and a half months but her poop didn't seem to change for ages. Up until nine or ten months everything seemed to come out as it went in—we'd just see little bits of carrot or red peppers in an otherwise liquidy, breast-fed poop. When she started to really dig into her food her stool gradually became much more solid."

Monica, mother of Alanna, 15 months

Eating Enough: Learning to Trust Your Baby

One of the hardest parts of BLW for many parents is trusting their baby to eat as much as she needs. The amounts BLW babies eat can continue to seem very small, even when they are beginning to eat purposefully (as opposed to just exploring), and it can be difficult to believe that they know what they are doing.

Parents who have been formula-feeding are used to having a fair amount of control over their baby's feedings and are generally guided on how much to give by the recommendations of the formula manufacturer, or by health professionals. Also, formula-fed babies generally have roughly the same amount of milk at each feeding. So if you are used to formula-feeding, it may take you a while to trust your baby to know how much and how often she needs to eat.

However, even parents who have been used to breast-feeding, and have already trusted their baby to eat and drink as much as she needs (without ever really knowing how much milk she is having) may find it hard to believe their baby is eating the "right" amount.

If you are worried that your baby is not eating enough, consider the following:

- Our ideas about how much babies should eat tend to be based on the old belief that a chubby baby was a healthy baby.
- Your baby is the expert on her own unique appetite and needs.
- You may be comparing the amount of solid food your BLW baby eats with the amount eaten by a baby fed on purées. Remember that puréed food is often mixed with water or milk, which makes it look much more than it really is—with BLW it's all food.
- Even babies of the same age, weight, and activity level may need to eat very different amounts because their metabolisms are different (we all know healthy adults who seem to live on thin air).
- Babies have small tummies (about the size of their fist); they need to eat little and often. They can't usually eat large amounts at every meal.
- The first solid foods are supposed to add to (or complement) the baby's milk diet, *not* to replace it. Breast milk or formula is still a baby's main source of nutrition in the early months of weaning and remains the most important part of their diet until they are at least a year old.

Sometimes it comes down to tricking yourself into feeling good about what your baby has eaten. If you give her a small amount of food, and she wants more, you'll be pleased. If you give her a large plateful and she can't manage it all you may be

BLW STORY

When Mia got to three or four months her grandparents were all saying that she should be eating solids. But Mia just wasn't interested—I really felt under pressure.

I tried offering food at six months but she'd just play with it—she wasn't even putting anything in her mouth at that age. I remember going out with some friends from my prenatal group and all the other babies were being spoon-fed a main course, a dessert, and then a little cookie to finish. And Mia wasn't eating anything—I was just breast-feeding. So, of course, I started to wonder if she was ever going to eat.

I wasn't very confident at that stage—I was worried that she was "just playing" and not really eating, but I just kept offering her something at every mealtime—and she gradually started eating. But even then 90 percent of it ended up on the floor; I don't think she got much inside her till about eight months. It took me quite a while to trust that she really could feed herself. I needed the confidence to know that if she's happy and growing and she's got the opportunity to eat then she's obviously not starving.

I just don't worry about it anymore. Some days she'll eat loads and then she might not eat anything much for a couple of days. But she really enjoys food now. She eats things that most babies probably don't even have the chance to try—like olives and chorizo and spicy foods. It's really good she's got such a broad palate already. Most people seem quite surprised. My Italian parents-in-law were very doubtful about the way we introduced her to solids—until we visited them for a meal and, at 11 months, Mia ate a whole bowlful of pasta.

Joanna, mother of Mia, 17 months

disappointed. But the chances are she will eat exactly the same amount—as much as she needs—whichever way you do it!

In general, if your baby is filling and wetting her diapers and healthy and thriving, then you can be confident that she is eating enough.

"When we talk about mealtimes my parents will say, 'Did you manage to get any food into Keira?' But it's not about getting food into her. Keira's quite capable of feeding herself so she's not going to starve; if she's hungry, and there's food, then she'll eat."   *Jennie, mother of Keira, 2*

Telling You She's Had Enough

Babies who are a few months into BLW usually give their parents clear signals that they don't want any more of a particular food, or that the meal is over. They may pick up individual pieces of food and drop them one by one over the edge of their high chair—or they may sweep everything off their tray. Some babies are more subtle: they simply start shaking their heads— or hand pieces of food to their parents. Some parents teach their babies sign language to help them communicate their needs. Either way, the message quickly becomes clear.

However, in the early stages of BLW it can be more difficult to tell when the baby has had enough, because throwing and dropping food are less purposeful. Luckily, in the early weeks you don't need to work out whether your baby has finished, since at this stage a "meal" is not really about eating at all—it's for learning about tastes and exploring food.

The key to ensuring that your baby has enough to eat is always to offer more—perhaps something different or something from your plate (even if it's the same as the food she has)—without any expectation that she will eat it. That way she can turn it down if she doesn't need it without you feeling disappointed. This is much safer than assuming that she's had enough just because her plate (or tray) is empty.

"Finn went through a phase of telling us he had had enough by clearing the tray himself—whole arm and hand extended like a windshield wiper. It was very effective and a clear signal he was done with that course. Since we have given him a plate or bowl he does the windshield wiping less and instead I ask him to place the bits on the plate. This often works as a distraction—but sometimes if he's fed up the whole plate will go!"

Mae'r, mother of Finn, 11 months

BLW STORY

I really enjoy watching Madeleine choosing what she's going to pick up; it's such a definite action when they pick it up themselves. We spoon-fed our first child, Noah, and I remember finding the mush stage really boring. After a while, offering the spoon and getting the shut mouth reply gets very tedious; I remember thinking that I'd rather do three diaper changes than one mealtime.

It's completely different with Madeleine. Because she's picking things up herself quite happily, you can see, at the start—when she's hungry—she's chewing everything quite quickly and getting it down. And then you can see her gradually slow down, until she starts playing with it and dropping it over the side of the high chair. It's the clear indication that "this meal's over, I've had enough."

Nick, father of Noah, 4, and Madeleine, 8 months

Food Fads

Closely linked to worries about *how much* young children eat are concerns about *what* they eat. Older babies and toddlers often go through phases of "finicky" eating when all they want is one particular food for days at a time. Although it can be baffling if your BLW baby suddenly wants to eat nothing but bananas, fads like this seem to be natural behavior; they shouldn't be confused with the fussiness seen in children who are using food as part of a battle of wills with their parents.

Babies and small children seem to know instinctively which foods will give them the nutrients they need, and many parents have noticed that "fads" coincide with their baby's general development or health; for example, babies and toddlers often seem to focus on carbohydrates during periods of rapid growth, or on protein foods, fruit, or milk feedings when recovering from an illness. In some cases, there are reports of babies completely refusing foods that they later turn out to be allergic to. If it really is babies' survival instinct that drives them to behave like this, it's no wonder they react so strongly when they are forced to eat something they don't want!

So it seems that it's not only natural for babies to "binge" on a single food (or a small group of foods) for several days—and then, quite suddenly, not want to eat those foods at all—it may actually be good for them. And it's unlikely they will become undernourished, since most foods contain several nutrients (not just one type) and very few need to be eaten every day.

Baby-led-weaning babies also show their preferences—and possibly their need—for certain foods by choosing what to eat first at each meal. Some parents have noticed that their children make a beeline for foods that are rich in fat when the weather is cold (fat is a concentrated source of calories, which are used up faster when the body needs to keep warm). Other babies go for meat first, or dark green vegetables—possibly when they need some extra iron.

> "I always felt I could tell the weather was turning colder
> when I found my children's fingerprints in the butter."
>
> *Mary, mother of two and grandmother of three*

Babies who crave a particular food seem to be responding to a need, so it's important to trust their instinct and let them make these choices. Allowing children to make decisions about food doesn't encourage them to become fussy; as we've seen, it's generally children who feel they have no control over their eating who are more likely to limit the foods they'll eat long-term.

Food fads are unpredictable, so don't assume that, just because your baby wanted nothing but mangoes yesterday, there's no point in offering her other foods today. Babies who are too young to talk can't ask for the foods they need; instead they show us what they want by choosing some foods—and turning down others—from the selection they are offered.

Just as your baby may binge on certain foods, she may "go off" a particular food, too—even one she previously liked. It's best to accept that this food may be rejected for quite a while. There's no need to worry about whether or not to include it in future meals; if it's on the family menu, just keep offering it (without pushing it). If she sees you eating it, and has the chance to try it again, there's every chance your baby will change her mind. But if you don't offer it, you won't know when she's ready to give it another try.

Above all, if your child goes through food fads, try to be relaxed about how extreme they seem to be and how long they last. This is easier said than done, but if you are finding yourself getting wound up about your baby's apparent refusal to eat anything except blueberries, ask yourself what the alternative is. Most mealtime battles don't start with a child refusing to eat but with a parent insisting that she does! Very few of these battles are won by the parents, and then only at the expense of a happy parent-child relationship. In other words, going to war with your child is not the answer. If they're allowed to run their course, food fads don't tend to last more than a few weeks at most.

> "I remember when Charlotte was ill with some sort of virus and all she ate was protein. It was bizarre. And on another occasion, we went on holiday when she was about two and a half, and all she ate was carbohydrate, and she grew about three centimeters in a couple of weeks. It was fascinating. I am a great believer that they will take what they need to suit their requirements."
>
> *Barbara, mother of Charlotte, 6,*
> *and David, 2*

> "Jacob went through a banana phase, when he would just eat a whole banana for breakfast every morning for about two weeks. And then of course one day, that was it, he didn't want banana any more. He'll have a little bit, but not like he used to."
>
> *Steve, father of Jacob, 8 months*

Drinks

As you are sharing your meals with your baby you may start to wonder if she should have a drink with her food, just like the grown-ups. If everyone else is drinking this will probably happen naturally; at some point your baby will become curi-ous and want to copy you drinking out of a glass, cup, or mug. As long as you aren't using something that could break if she bit it (such as a wineglass), or drinking something unsuitable (such as alcohol), just let her try. Babies quickly learn how to drink out of an open cup if they are allowed to practice (see page 162). However, as with your baby's first experiences with food, it's only when she's done it a few times that she will work out that drinking quenches her thirst.

How soon your baby actually *needs* extra drinks depends to some extent on whether you are breast-feeding or formula-feeding. Fully breast-fed babies can get everything they need in the way of food and drink, even in very hot weather, just by deciding how often to feed and for how long, because breast milk changes throughout a feeding. This process can continue working well into the weaning period, provided the baby is allowed to breast-feed whenever she asks. If you give her the chance to have a drink of water with her meals she will learn about it in just the same way as she learns about food.

Formula-fed babies' milk is too rich to be really thirst-quenching and doesn't change throughout the feeding, so they need to be offered drinks of water occasionally even before they start on solids. Offering your baby water regularly (prefer-ably in a cup) will help her (and you) to recognize when she is thirsty rather than hungry, while also making sure she doesn't put on too much weight (a risk if she repeatedly has calorie-rich formula when all she really needs is a drink). She doesn't have to drink the water, but she should be given the choice.

Water and breast milk are the best drinks for babies and young children. Tap water is fine—preferably filtered—and it doesn't need to be boiled once your baby is over six months. Pure fruit (or vegetable) juice (diluted with plenty of water: at least 10 parts water to one part juice) is okay in *very* small quantities, but it can damage teeth (even before they come through) if drunk too often, and it can give babies a taste for sweet drinks. Bear in mind that fruit juice is never as nutritious as the whole fruit—it can also fill a baby up and take the place of more nourishing food. If you do want to give your baby diluted juice, using an open cup will be better for her teeth than drinking from a spouted cup or a bottle. But the best option is to stick to water, which she will drink if she's thirsty.

Commercial fruit drinks tend to have a lot of sugar and almost no nourishment and are best avoided completely. Tea is not good for babies as it can make them less able to absorb some of the nutrients from their food, especially iron. Coffee, tea, and cola drinks also contain caffeine, which can make babies and children irritable. Cows' milk is not recommended as a drink for children under a year old (see page 123).

Dropping Milk Feedings

Babies grow more in their first year than at any other time in their lives, and they need nutrient- and calorie-rich breast milk or formula to do this; solid foods—whatever they are—don't contain anywhere near as much nourishment. So don't be surprised if your baby shows no signs of wanting to replace her milk feedings with solids for several months after taking her first mouthful of food.

As we've seen, when babies first start eating solid foods all they are really doing is discovering different tastes and textures and allowing their bodies to adjust gradually to digesting new foods. As they begin to eat more at mealtimes, the need for breast milk or formula gets less; how fast this happens varies enormously from baby to baby (see page 141).

How you and your baby experience the gradual cutting down of milk feedings will also differ depending on whether you are breast-feeding or formula-feeding. If you are breast-feeding and letting her have all her drinks at the breast you may not notice any change in the number of feedings she has each day, though they may be shorter. If you are formula-feeding, you can expect her to be having only one or two milk feedings a day by the time she is a year old.

If you have been combining breast-feeding with formula-feeding you will probably find that you can cut out the formula and keep the breast-feeding going. Doing it this way will ensure that you and your child benefit for longer from the health advantages that come with breast-feeding.

Whether you are breast-feeding, formula-feeding, or doing a bit of both, it's best, at first, to think of milk feedings and mealtimes as two different things. In the early days, if your baby is hungry she wants (and needs) milk. She has no idea that other foods can fill her up, and she won't enjoy being sat in a high chair and given pieces of food to play with when what she really wants is her milk. Thinking of milk feedings as something separate will also mean that reducing them will happen naturally as your baby's need for them gets less.

As your baby begins to eat more at each mealtime, she will either ask for her next milk feeding slightly later than usual or she will take less milk. When she is eating real little meals and having a drink of water (or a short breast-feed) with them, she will simply begin to miss out some of her main milk feedings altogether. As long as you listen to what she is "telling" you (if she wants milk she'll ask for it in her usual way; if she doesn't, she'll turn away when offered the breast or bottle), and don't try to make her take more or less milk than she wants, you should be able to rely on her appetite to let you both know what to do.

"Luke's probably dropped one feeding—if not two—
already. But when he first started solids he would often
want milk afterward, and I remember saying: 'He wants
more milk now than he did before.' But I think that was
a phase after the new food. Breast-feeding is so dependent on other things—whether he's tired, or teething, or
feeling poorly. If he's tired, he'll often have some dinner
and go straight on the boob, just all at once."

Anna, mother of Luke, 8 months

The way your baby cuts down her milk feedings can also
work in reverse, so it's very flexible. There may be days when
she is less interested in solid foods, or when, for whatever
reason, you aren't able to give her as many meals as usual.
Or it may be that she's not feeling well or is teething, and
wants the comfort of a milk feeding. On those days, her
appetite for milk will increase, so that she doesn't go hungry.
If you are formula-feeding, you'll simply need to let her have
more formula; if you are breast-feeding, allowing her to feed
as often as she wants will stimulate your body to make more
milk—even if your supply had already begun to lessen.

"I didn't notice much change in the breast-feeding. The
food was just on top of the breast milk, and Austin
seemed to increase the amount of calories he was
getting from food very, very gradually. He's a big boy,
Austin. I don't know if that's got anything to do with it."

Bryony, mother of Austin, 22 months

"When we started we just kept going with the same
amount of formula. It didn't seem to change for ages
and we seemed to be doing nothing but feeding, with
either formula or solids—and then when Chloe was

about nine months she just forgot to ask for her after-
noon bottle one day—so I didn't remind her. She didn't
seem to miss that bottle and didn't go back to it. I was
really surprised—I thought I'd have to decide more for
her because I was bottle-feeding."

Helen, mother of Chloe, 15 months

ENDING MILK FEEDINGS

The natural conclusion to BLW is for the baby to decide when
to stop having milk feedings. In practice, this way of complet-
ing the changeover to full family meals is more common for
babies who are breast-fed than for those who are bottle-fed—
largely because parents are advised to switch their baby from
a bottle to a cup by the time she is a year old (prolonged
bottle-feeding has been shown to lead to tooth decay). Most
choose to phase out formula milk at the same time. It is very
unusual for a baby to spontaneously give up breast-feeding
before her first birthday. Many children (and their mothers)
continue to enjoy the nurturing and health protection that
breast-feeding provides until they are well into toddlerhood,
even if it's just first thing in the morning and at bedtime.

Breast-feeding protects babies from many different infections
(for example, chest, ear, and stomach infections) and the longer
a mother continues to feed her baby the greater her protection
against illnesses such as breast and ovarian cancer and oste-
oporosis. The World Health Organization recommends that all
children should be breast-fed for two years or more.

A breast-fed baby will let her mother know when she is
ready to give up breast-feeding, either by not asking for the
breast or by repeatedly turning away when it is offered. If she
is old enough to talk she may simply tell her that she doesn't
want to breast-feed any more.

Breakfast, Lunch, and Dinner—
Plus Snacks

Once your baby decides to cut down on milk feedings, she may also be hungry between meals. Human babies are natural "grazers." That is, they naturally eat little and often. It's only as we get older that we train ourselves to eat large meals infrequently (though whether this is a good thing is open to debate). Babies' stomachs are far too small to be limited to three meals a day, especially once they are having fewer milk feedings. Most babies simply haven't got the capacity to eat enough to keep them going for four or five hours during the day without food.

So, once your baby has really gotten going with solids and is asking for fewer or smaller milk feedings, you can start to offer her healthy snacks. Allowing her to eat good food, little and often, also has the advantage of making you less likely to worry when the amount she eats at "official" mealtimes is small. Remember, though, that it's only by offering that you can find out what your baby wants; don't push her to have a snack if she wants milk.

For a baby under about 18 months, there's no need to make a distinction between snacks and meals, either in relation to where and when they happen or in terms of how big they are—just so long as they are nutritious and, between them, they give the baby the chance to eat something from all the main food groups each day (see page 185). Young children should continue to be offered food (either snacks or meals) as many as six or more times a day for several years. Offering frequent nutritious snacks is also one of the best ways to prevent young children asking for sweets and junk food. But remember that, as with her meals, if your baby turns down an offered snack she is simply telling you she doesn't need it.

Many foods marketed as snacks are not healthy. Often adults and older children will reach for foods such as candy bars and sodas when they feel irritable or hungry. These foods are not good for anyone: babies, children, or adults. Usually heavy in salt and/or sugar, as well as additives, they provide a short-term energy rush with very little actual nourishment. Sugary foods are bad for teeth at all ages—even before baby teeth have come through.

Since many possess no real nutritional value, these highly processed snack foods should be given only if your child is hungry and absolutely nothing else is available. Making sure you have snack foods such as an apple, banana, or rice cake with you whenever you are out should make these occasions rare (see page 117 for ideas for snacks). If you do need to let your baby have foods that have little nutritional value, try to keep the amount to a minimum so that she isn't so full that she can't manage her next meal. A whole packet of potato chips may not seem that much to you, but it's enough to fill a toddler's tummy.

SAFE SNACKING

Snacks should be treated exactly the same way as mealtimes in terms of safety. Make sure your baby is sitting up (supported if necessary) when she is eating or handling food, and that an adult is with her at all times. Don't let your child eat snacks (or meals) while she is watching TV—she needs to concentrate if she is to eat safely and to recognize when she's had enough.

Many of the foods that you will be offering your baby at mealtimes can work just as well as a snack, and thinking of all your baby's snacks as mini-meals will help you to choose nutritious foods to give her, whatever the time of day. Nutritious snacks add to your baby's well-being—it's only nonnutritious ones that are a problem.

Picnics

Baby-led weaning works particularly well for picnics. Most picnic food is designed to be eaten with fingers, which is exactly what your baby is used to doing. There are no concerns about mess and there's usually no hurry, so it can be even easier to share a picnic than a meal at the table.

You don't have to go far to have a picnic—your garden or the local park will do fine—and if the weather is bad, you could even have one indoors.

6.

Baby-Led Weaning and Family Life

"Baby-led weaning is great for babies and for families. Mealtimes are about social interaction as well as eating, and BLW promotes this from the beginning. I always encourage parents to try it; most love it and their babies have fun!"   *Alison, specialist public health nurse*

"When Ellie got to about 18 months I realized I was beginning to nag her about food. Not cajoling exactly, but asking her if she'd really finished and didn't she want to try a bit of chicken, etc. And I started to think she wasn't eating enough. I have to keep reminding myself that she still knows what she needs. It's just so ingrained, having to persuade children to eat, and mixing up eating with 'good' and 'bad' behavior."

Sharon, mother of Ellie, 22 months

Maintaining a Baby-Led Approach

As your child grows it's important to make sure that mealtimes are still enjoyable. Toddlers have a bad reputation when it comes to food, but it's not inevitable for small children to be picky eaters and badly behaved at the table—it's just so common that it seems as if it must be normal. There's no need to panic when you hear the horror stories; BLW really can help to prevent many of the problems parents encounter with toddlers and food.

Small children want to assert their will and become more self-reliant and independent and your child will be happiest where he can succeed on his own and have a sense of achievement. Baby-led weaning is perfect for this—as long as you keep the hands-off approach. So continue to trust your child's appetite, give him only as much help as he genuinely needs, and let him progress at his own pace.

Silverware

Once your child has had enough time to become a skilled self-feeder you may start to wonder about his table manners. But there's no need to worry: he won't always eat with his fingers and get covered in food; small children have a strong drive to copy those around them, so unless *you* always eat with your hands the chances are he'll soon want to experiment with a knife and fork. When you include him in your meals, *really* include him, and as soon as he has learned the basics of eating, set a place for him with his own utensils. Choose a child-sized set, though—asking a child to use adult-sized silverware is the equivalent of expecting an adult to eat with salad servers!

As with food, it's best not to expect too much of your baby too soon. To start with he will see his cutlery as part of playing and copying, not as a way to get food into his mouth. For that, his fingers will be a lot more efficient. Eventually, in his own time, he'll work out what to do with a fork or spoon (using a knife will take quite a bit longer). Trying to encourage, force, or "teach" him to use silverware before he is ready will only upset and frustrate him.

Some babies attempt to use a fork or spoon only occasionally for many months because they know they'll get more food if they use their hands; others get the hang of it very quickly. Most babies, though, are beginning to use a spoon or fork by their first birthday. As long as you let him have plenty of practice with different textures and shapes your baby will learn to manage his utensils efficiently, at his own pace.

Although most parents give their baby a spoon to start with, many babies find a fork easier to use in the beginning. Spoons work best in a bowl, with sloppy food—as you know from feeding yourself. Getting food on to a spoon from a flat plate can be difficult, and keeping it on the spoon while you get it to your mouth is quite tricky, too. Forks are much easier to load than spoons because spearing a piece of food is usually easier than scooping it up, and the food tends to stay on a fork even if it's turned upside down. So you may want to go for a fork, initially, rather than a spoon. The fork you choose doesn't have to be one designed for a baby, but it should be small enough for him to manage, with prongs that are not so thick that they crush the food, nor so thin or pointed that they could cause an injury.

Working out how to use a "dipper" (such as a carrot, crust, or breadstick, see page 113) in foods like hummus or yogurt can often help a baby learn to use spoons. And babies can take food off a spoon with their mouths before they are able to load one themselves, so handing your baby a ready-loaded spoon can also be a useful way of showing him how a spoon works. But don't be surprised if, the first few times, he turns the spoon upside down and loses everything on it—or flings the food across the room when he waves his arm. Your baby doesn't know this is going to happen until he's done it a few times— and even then it will be a long time before he understands that it actually *matters* if food is thrown around! So expect some mess—or, if the weather is fine, let his early experiments with spoons happen outside!

"Oliver always had a teaspoon at mealtimes, even before he started eating, just so he could join in. At about 11 months I bought him his own set of silverware, and he just copied us. At first I would put some cereal on to a spoon and then hand it to him. He was good at getting it to his mouth, because he could see me eating my cereal at the same time. And he'd use his hands, too, which was fine. Now, though, he wants to use the big silverware."   *Carmel, mother of Oliver, 14 months*

When your child *does* start to use silverware (rather than just play with it), he'll be very slow. So take a deep breath, and be patient. It can be agonizing to watch a young child attempt, time after time, to get a piece of food on to his fork or spoon and then, once he has managed it, to see it fall off on the way to his mouth. Your baby will do this many, many times before he masters cutlery. Try not to interfere or "help" him too much—however hard it seems to be for him—he'll learn faster if he is allowed to work it out for himself. Your baby's personality will dictate how quickly he gets frustrated and goes back to using his fingers for the rest of the meal, but, if he's the patient, tenacious type, meals could take some time.

"Mason will spend absolutely ages working very hard to use his silverware. He uses the fork to try to stab the food, and often, rather than eating it himself, he will then offer it to me. He occasionally manages to get it into his own mouth as well, but he's still really learning to do it. So our meal-times have become a bit more leisurely recently. He goes back to his hands sometimes, but he's surprisingly persistent with his cutlery." *Jo, mother of Mason, 16 months*

Key points

- Forks are easier than spoons at first.
- Handing your baby a ready-loaded spoon will help him to learn how it works.
- Encouraging your baby to use a dipper with soft foods (see page 113) introduces the idea of using a spoon.
- Setting a place for your baby with a spoon and fork whenever he joins you at the table will mean he can start to use them when he's ready.
- You'll need to be patient when your child starts to use silverware, because his progress will probably be quite slow. (If you try to teach him or encourage him you'll probably both get frustrated.)
- It's better not to interfere or "help" your child unless he asks you to.
- It's important to be a good role model—if your child sees you eating with silverware he'll be more inclined to want to use it himself.

PLAYING AT BEING SPOON-FED

Toddlers are naturally playful and enjoy sharing and taking turns. Once he is old enough your child may want to spoon-feed you—or even ask you to spoon-feed him. This is not a sign that he's regressing, or that he has missed out on being spoon-fed—and it doesn't mean he'll want you to feed him all the time. It's just a game.

"Rosie's a neat little eater now, even though it was so messy to start with. She sits very nicely and really understands that meals are sociable settings."

Stacey, mother of Grace, 4, and Rosie, 14 months

Cups

Your baby will probably be curious about cups as soon as he starts on solids, if not before. So, once he is sharing meals with you it's probably a good idea to start offering him water in his own cup.

Although trainer or "sippy" cups (with a spout) can be very useful when you are out and about because they reduce the risk of spills, it's a good idea to let your baby practice with a real cup when you're at home. It will be messier initially, but he'll learn faster.

Babies need to work out how to tip a cup up just enough to be able to drink, but not so much that they get wet. Cups that are slanted are designed for babies to learn about tipping; they need to be tipped less than standard cups and the baby has a clearer view of what's in the cup and what happens when it's tipped. However, you don't have to start with a slanted cup—many babies manage very well with a standard cup from the beginning.

An important thing to consider is the *width* of the cup you give to your baby: a wide-rimmed cup is the equivalent, for a baby, of an adult trying to drink out of a small bucket—you only have to tip it a little and most of the liquid goes down the sides of your chin! A play tea or coffee cup, a medicine cup or a shot-sized glass may be a better "fit" for your baby's mouth.

Babies often find a full cup easier to manage than a half-full one to start with, because it doesn't need to be tipped up as far. If you choose a small cup, which needs only a small amount of water to fill it, there will be less to mop up when it gets spilled.

Babies learn by exploring and experimenting. They can't be expected to know what happens when a cup is tipped up if they haven't been allowed to try, and they don't know that pouring water over the table matters. Allowing your baby to practice pouring games at the sink or in the bath can help him to learn how a cup works and may mean he needs to experiment less at the table.

Part of exploring, for your baby, may involve his finding out what can be put into a cup as well as what comes out of it. He may be fascinated to discover which foods float and which ones sink. While adults may not like their drinks to taste of sprouts or fish, this is unlikely to worry your baby. (It's a good idea, though, to take out any small pieces of food, such as peas, before he drinks, to minimize the risk of choking.) Once he has made his discoveries he won't need to experiment so much.

Table Manners

Many parents (and grandparents) worry that a baby who is allowed to play with his food and feed himself with his fingers will never learn proper table manners. Anecdotal evidence suggests that it's babies who are *not* allowed to experiment with food who are more likely to behave badly at the table when they are older.

Early self-feeding is about exploration and learning. Babies need time to acquire the basic skills before they can start to think about fine-tuning their actions to fit in with their parents' ideas of polite behavior. And they need to be included in family mealtimes as much as possible, so that they get to see how others behave.

You are the most important role model for your child, so you need to make sure you are a reliable one. If you want him to behave well when you take him to a restaurant then you need to model that behavior at home. Even when you are at home, try to be consistent about how you eat each type of food. It's obviously fine to hold a sandwich in your hand to eat it, but if you sometimes eat french fries with a knife and fork and sometimes with your fingers, then expect your child to do the same—wherever he is. Children younger than about seven years old can't be expected to understand the subtleties of behaving differently on different occasions or in different settings.

There's no need to praise your child for behaving well or scold him for bad behavior. Young children have a natural desire to copy others and to do what they think is expected of them—if your child senses that he has surprised you by behaving well he will be confused about what he is expected to do. All you need to do is trust him, give him time, and set a good example, and his table manners shouldn't present a problem.

How to encourage good table manners

- Whenever possible, eat with your baby.
- Be a good role model—and be consistent.
- Don't scold or praise your child—simply trust him to behave well.

"Caroline was always a very sociable eater; she would quite happily come to a restaurant with us and sit and eat whatever it was we were eating. I remember her eating monkfish and prawns, just after she was a year

old. The whole experience of sharing a meal seemed
quite important to her."

Bethany, mother of Caroline, 6,
and Daniel, 2

Eating Out

Eating out as a family is one of the great joys of BLW. In the
early months you don't have to worry about taking along preprepared purées and asking harassed waiters to provide bowls
of hot water to heat them up—and you don't have to watch
your food get cold while you feed your baby. Most restaurants
will have something on the menu that he can eat, although at
first it will probably be easier just to share your own meal with
him.

Many cafés and restaurants will provide a child's portion (or
an appetizer-size portion) of an adult dish if you ask them.
Alternatively, if you ask for an extra plate (or bring your own)
you could share a main dish with your child. Lots of dishes are
suitable—from spaghetti and meatballs to the most elaborate
restaurant food—especially once he's past the first few months
of solids. You'll soon get a feel for what he can manage.

Ordering a range of starter-size portions of main dishes for
all of you to share can be great fun for your child, giving him
the opportunity to try lots of new tastes. Turkish mezze (pita
bread, hummus, marinated peppers, etc.) and Spanish tapas
can usually be eaten easily with fingers and are good for sharing. Pizza and pasta are also easy to share, and most children
love them. Allowing your baby to choose from what everyone
else is eating can be easier than trying to decide on a separate
dish for him.

"A friend and I went for lunch with our babies when they were about 10 months old. We ordered lots of appetizers that we could all share and that they could eat easily with their hands and we just put it on the table. It was brilliant; we were chatting and the two babies were grabbing bits of food and entertaining themselves. We were completely relaxed."

Chantelle, mother of Abby, 2

As your baby grows you'll realize there is no need to turn to the "kids' menu" in restaurants or limit your choice of where to eat to places serving "child-friendly" food. Your child will be used to normal, nutritious family food and, as long as he's been given plenty of variety of tastes, he'll probably be quite adventurous. So you won't have to resort to processed chicken nuggets and chips because "that's all he'll eat." Most so-called "kids' food" is high in salt, sugar, and additives, all of which are bad for children. What they need are small portions of nutritious adult meals; the longer you can protect your child from junk food the better.

Not all restaurants clean their high chairs thoroughly, so you may want to take along some antibacterial wipes to use on the chair before you put your child into it—especially if he has not yet mastered eating off a plate. Be aware that it's not just the tray you need to clean—the child who used the chair last will probably have smeared her dinner in all the places your child finds to put his! Some parents also take along their baby's own roll-up placemat so that they can be confident he is eating off a clean surface (see page 88).

"When mine were little I always carried disposable baby wipes with me wherever we went. You never know when you'll need them, whether it's wiping sticky fingers, grubby tables, or dirty bottoms. Even now, if something gets spilled, my children always expect me to have a baby wipe on me."

Diana, mother of Abigail, 14, and Bethany, 12

If you eat out a lot it may be a good idea to buy a clamp-on seat that can be fixed to most types of table. These are useful if a restaurant has a limited number of high chairs and it means your baby will sit up at the table with everyone else, so he feels included. A toddler may prefer to kneel on a normal chair or use a booster seat rather than sit in a high chair. As long as you can make it safe for him, there's no reason why he can't eat like this.

Staying at the table

Deciding what to give your child to eat in a restaurant is fairly easy, but once he is walking confidently you may find you need to employ a few tactics to keep him happy in his high chair. Meals in a restaurant or café usually last much longer than they do at home, and there can be long gaps between courses. Children get bored quickly, especially if they don't have their parents' full attention because they're busy chatting.

Toddlers are naturally curious about their surroundings; your child will probably find this new environment fascinating and want to explore. He can't be expected to sit still for long periods with nothing to do before the meal arrives or after he's finished eating. After all, you don't normally keep him waiting 20 minutes for his food without allowing him to play, and he can't be expected to understand that eating out has different rules from eating at home. Taking him for a walk around the restaurant or outside will keep him amused—and make him less likely to protest during the meal because he's spotted something he desperately wants to explore.

Thinking ahead, and seeing eating out from your child's point of view, will help you to avoid the most common problems.

Tips for keeping meals out stress-free

- Order your child's meal as soon as you can—if it comes with the starters he'll probably still be happily eating it when the main dishes arrive. Relax and let him eat at his own pace, regardless of which course everyone else is eating.
- Delay sitting your child at the table until the meal is about to arrive (or has arrived and cooled down), perhaps by taking him for a walk.
- Take along some small toys, or a coloring book and crayons, to keep your child occupied at the table.
- Check that the food and the plate aren't too hot—it's a good idea to ask the waiter to put your child's plate in the middle of the table rather than in front of him, so you can check it before he grabs anything.
- Let your child feed himself—and resist the temptation to make him eat more than he wants, or taste something he doesn't want to, no matter how much you're paying for it.
- Take along his own cup, so you don't have to worry about how he will manage a big restaurant glass (or whether he might break it). It's handy if your child can drink out of a straw. Most babies can manage this by the time they reach a year old, provided they've been given the opportunity to learn.
- If your child likes to use (or play with) utensils, take his own set with you.

- If you are worried about the mess, take along your own splash mat, or pick up the bits from the high chair and the floor once your child has finished eating.

> "We really enjoy going out for meals, and Brendan eats
> well in restaurants. We try to order very quickly and then
> one of us will usually just go for a walk with him, either
> around the restaurant or outside the restaurant along the
> street; we try not to sit him in the high chair until the
> food arrives. He's not very easily entertained with toys in
> restaurants but he will usually sit very nicely as soon as
> the food is in front of him."
>
> Maxine, *mother of Brendan, 17 months*

Self-Service

Older babies and small children usually enjoy serving themselves at the table, and putting everything into serving dishes can be one of the best ways to help you resist the temptation to decide how much food should be on your child's plate. It also encourages conversation and sharing and, if you have already gone into battle with your child over food, it's a good way to help you all to enjoy mealtimes again.

Allowing your child to serve himself helps him to judge his own appetite; most children are surprisingly accurate when they're allowed to decide in advance roughly how much they are going to eat. So, rather than putting your child's portion straight on to his plate, try letting him serve himself. He may need a little help to manage serving spoons, but let him choose what to have and how much to take. (But remember that he'll copy what you do, so keep an eye on the saltshaker and the salsa!)

As well as helping him judge his appetite, dishing up his own food will give your child valuable lessons in hand-eye coordination, muscle control, measuring, and judging distance and volume. It will also provide him with a sense of control and achievement, and will make him feel (and be) more independent. Salads and other cold dishes are ideal to start with. If the food is hot make sure he can't burn or scald himself, especially if it's something sloppy such as soup or a casserole.

"Sallyann wants to join in with cooking; she enjoys peeling and cutting and putting things in the pan and stirring them; she even wipes the table. She insists on pouring her own gravy and loves to scrape the pan for second helpings. If we have a casserole she picks bits out and tells us if they are nice."

Anthony, father of Sallyann, 3

Small children often like to help themselves to snacks from the cupboard or fridge, too. It can be a good idea to have a small tray of healthy snack foods, in containers that your child can open easily, or a fruit bowl that he can reach. If you do encourage your child to help himself to snacks, teach him to sit down and eat his snack with you—running around playing while eating can be a choking hazard and small children should never eat unsupervised.

"If Hayley is hungry, she just goes into the kitchen and points at the fridge or goes to the fruit bowl and gets an apple or something—she doesn't have to wait until it's lunchtime. And we don't have any unhealthy snacks in the house—so she can have whatever she wants."

Serena, mother of Hayley, 2

Toddlers often notice what other children are eating at play-groups and nurseries and may want the same food. It's best not to make too much of a fuss, even if the food is unhealthy; the odd cookie won't do any harm, and making certain foods forbidden will only make them more desirable. If your child is used to healthy food at home, he's more likely to make healthy choices when he's out.

> "Lexie was at a party recently and was helping herself to food. She took a piece of chocolate cake and left most of it. Then she filled her bowl with blueberries and when she'd eaten them all, she went back for more—she just wasn't bothered by all the cakes and cookies."
>
> *Harriet, mother of Lexie, 22 months*

Bribes, Rewards, and Punishments

As your child gets older it can be tempting to use food as a reward for good behavior, as a bribe to persuade him to do something he doesn't want to do, or even—by withdrawing certain foods—as a punishment. But linking food with behavior rather than with appetite will distort his attitude to food—as well as spelling disaster for the management of his behavior long-term.

Treats for being good may seem harmless enough, but bear in mind that the reward you (or other members of the family) choose to give is unlikely to be a plate of vegetables or a banana—it's much more likely to be chocolates, cookies, or candy. Your child will very quickly begin to see these foods as especially desirable and come to expect them whenever he's well-behaved. There are three potential problems here: your child may begin to see chocolate and sweets as "better" than other foods, he may start to eat more sugary foods than you would like him to have, and he may start to behave well only because he wants some cake!

Using food as a bribe or punishment presents similar problems. Once you start saying things such as: "If you eat your carrots we can go to the playground," or "If you don't finish your sprouts you won't get any dessert," your child will very quickly become suspicious of vegetables, be convinced they are absolutely second best to dessert, or see eating them as a chore to be endured before something better comes along. There's no reason why children shouldn't choose to save a little bit of room for dessert, just as adults do. If you don't want your child to have dessert in preference to a savory dish, it's better not to include it in the meal.

Bribery, rewards, and punishment confuse food with power and control; they're the opposite of what BLW is all about because they interfere with a child's instinct to know what he needs. And using food in this way doesn't work long term anyway: children quickly see through these ploys and discover ways to regain the control for themselves.

> "Tom's nearly four, and he's got lots of friends whose parents are still spoon-feeding them at times. They are having to do what they were doing when their children were six months old—nudging them along, and saying, 'You'll get treats if you finish your broccoli'—all that kind of stuff. It's so much easier if you just treat it in a matter-of-fact way: 'It's dinnertime, just eat what you want to eat and don't eat anything you don't want to eat.'"
>
> *Phil, father of Tom, 4*

FOOD AND COMFORT

It can be tempting to give children sweet treats to cheer them up when they're crying or upset, but in reality all these treats do is bribe them to stop crying. A cuddle and a kiss are what they really need. Repeatedly using food to comfort children risks them confusing the two—and may make them more prone, as adults, to seek out sweet things whenever they feel miserable.

Avoiding the Emotional Battleground

Most mealtime battles with toddlers are the result of a mismatch over what the parent thinks the child needs and what *he* thinks he needs. With BLW this shouldn't happen, as long as the parents continue to trust their child's appetite.

Children have a strong survival instinct, especially where food is concerned. They have an extremely reliable sense of *when* they need to eat, *what* to eat, and *how much*. It is up to their parents to trust them. Sometimes parents find it hard to believe that an active 18-month-old only needs to eat as much as he did at nine months (or even less)—especially as he was probably having more milk feedings at nine months than he is now. But babies need an extraordinary amount of calories in their first year because their rate of growth is so fast. Although it seems as though toddlers are shooting up, they are not growing at the same rate as they were when they were younger, so they don't necessarily need more food. In fact, if a baby ate as much in his second year as he did in his first, he would be absolutely huge!

There is no more need to worry about your child's eating now than when he was younger; if he is well and thriving, he knows what he needs. Just make sure the meals you offer are nutritious and well balanced, and that he's not filling up on milk, juice, or nonnutritious snacks (especially once he is better at making his demands known). Most important of all, remember to keep mealtimes relaxed and enjoyable. It's very easy for them to become a battle of wills between parents and child, but battles almost always lead to the child eating even less of the foods the parents want him to eat.

Tips for keeping toddler mealtimes safe, relaxed and enjoyable:

- Continue to trust your child's appetite—it's his tummy, and he knows what he needs.
- Remind yourself that he may eat less than he did when he was a baby because his growth rate is slower now.
- Make sure he doesn't fill up on milk, juice, or nonnutritious snacks between meals.
- Let him serve himself as much as possible at the table.
- If you allow him to help himself to snacks, teach him to sit down while he eats.
- Avoid using food as a reward, punishment, or bribe.
- Don't give food in place of comfort.

"As soon as Paige turned two my mom decided it was time we stopped letting her 'have her own way' with food. She'd pretend she was going to eat Paige's dinner if she didn't finish it, and say: 'You're not going to waste all that yummy food, are you?' It was just habit, from feeding her own kids, and it was good-natured— she wasn't trying to bully Paige. But Paige started to be a bit difficult at the table, pushing her food away and so on—but only when Granny was there."

Danielle, mother of Paige, 3

BLW STORY

Baby-led weaning is so easy. Lidia is always happy to sit and feed herself, and she really enjoys mealtimes. Recently a friend asked me to spoon-feed a little girl she was looking after. I couldn't do it—even though I spoon-fed my oldest daughter years ago. It made me feel really uncomfortable after doing BLW with Lidia. The baby was a year old—perfectly capable of feeding herself—and it seemed so wrong. It almost felt like force-feeding.

It feels so much more natural to trust your baby and let them get on with it. Feeding Lidia this way has changed all my ideas about mealtimes for the coming years. With Jo, my oldest daughter, I was always saying, "Eat up your dinner," and she remembers it. I feel really mean about that now. You just can't do that with BLW. That's a big change of mind-set; I was brought up to believe you can't leave anything on your plate.

I feel much more relaxed at mealtimes with Lidia, and I think that will last throughout her childhood, because I've accepted that she decides how hungry she is and what she wants to eat. I'm not going to make mealtimes a battle, and that's really a positive thing.

Lucy, mother of Jo, 16, and Lidia, 17 months

Going Back to Work

Organizing child care when you return to work after parental leave can be challenging. However, BLW shouldn't present any extra problems as long as you take the time to ensure your child care provider—whether it's relatives, a nanny, or day care staff—understands the concept so they can follow BLW safely.

Most child care providers are very open to BLW, especially once they see it in action. It's common for grandparents, especially, to be doubtful at the outset and then, after seeing their grandchildren feed themselves, say that they regret not knowing about BLW when their own children were babies. However, the person who will be caring for your baby may have spent years introducing babies to solids using spoon-feeding and may not understand why you aren't happy for them to feed your baby the "normal" way when he's with them. If they haven't seen a baby of six or seven months feed himself, they could even be afraid to let your child handle real food.

> "Looking back, I think a big advantage of BLW was for my parents, who have cared for Natalya while I worked since she was a baby. I know for them it meant that there was no additional food to produce other than extra quantities to feed an extra mouth. I think they were surprised at how simple it was."
>
> *Julie, mother of Natalya, 4*

If they have had children of their own it's also worth reminding them that they would have encouraged their babies to start finger foods from about six months and would have expected them to be beginning to be able to chew at that age.

All you are doing (and asking them to do) is to miss out on the purée stage.

> "People have a picture in their mind of a baby starting solids, and for a lot of people, that picture is of a lying-back 16-week-old baby. But when you explain that you're not talking about that baby, you're talking about an older baby who can sit up and pick things up and chew, it begins to make sense to them."
>
> *Katie, mother of Sammy, 5, and Elvis, 2*

If you are leaving your baby in the care of someone else, it's important to make sure they understand that, at the beginning, mealtimes are for learning and playing, and that few babies eat anything at all in the first few weeks. They may find that your baby takes quite a while to get going with food and are less likely to be concerned if you've explained that this is normal.

Babies and children sometimes become less adventurous with food when they are going through periods of stress or transition, so it's quite possible that, for the first few weeks after you go back to work, your baby will want only familiar foods. He may even lose his appetite for anything but milk feedings. Once he has settled into the new routine, however, he'll go back to being his usual self.

It's important to make sure your baby's caregiver understands that they shouldn't offer your baby solid food when he is hungry for a milk feeding.

Your baby should be offered a small selection of foods and allowed to do what he wants with them. There is no need to put food into his hand—and pieces should certainly not be put into his mouth. Explain that sticks or fingers of food will be easiest for him to manage at first. (Many child care professionals assume they should cut food into bite-size chunks, as they would for a toddler who is using silverware.) It may be a good idea if you prepare your baby's food in advance—just until his caregiver can see what sorts of shapes are good and which foods are okay to offer.

> "Sometimes Amy's day care provider would give her things chopped up too small, and Amy couldn't pick them up. It was just habit. If you've weaned 10 kids like she had, the old-fashioned way, you automatically think about purées, followed by mash and then small pieces. The idea that the pieces need to be very large was a completely new way of thinking about it for her."
>
> *Alex, mother of Amy, 21 months*

Make sure they know that you want your baby to be allowed to take his time over his food and that you *really* mean it when you say it doesn't matter how much or how little he eats—most grandmothers, nannies, and babysitters would feel they were neglecting a basic duty if they didn't make sure a child they were caring for ate as much as *they* thought he should.

> "I'd pick Kylie up, and her day care teacher would say, 'She did eat, but it was more me feeding her, she didn't seem that keen.' I kept saying, 'It doesn't matter if she doesn't eat anything'—but it's so ingrained, that worry they're not getting enough food."
>
> *Marcie, mother of Kylie, 2*

It's best if your day care provider knows in advance that your baby will drop a lot of his food so that you can work out together how they will deal with this—both in terms of managing the mess and of being sure that only food that has been dropped onto a clean surface is handed back to him.

Your baby's caregiver needs to understand about gagging (see page 46), and how to recognize it (many people confuse it with choking, and panic unnecessarily). Make sure they understand why it is important for babies to be sitting upright and to have someone with them while they are handling food, and why it's the baby who should be in control of what goes into his mouth. Those who are looking after other children as well need to be alert to the danger of older children putting food into the baby's mouth. (Anyone caring for babies and small children should have basic training in first aid.)

Whoever is looking after your child would probably appreciate any BLW tips you have discovered. It's also good to update them as his abilities and tastes develop—and ask them to do the same for you.

> "I was expressing breast milk at work, so I could see that I was producing less milk, very gradually, as the months went on. By the time Olivia was 11 months, I was only producing a couple of ounces in a day. So I reckoned I could probably stop the expressing and she could make it up in the evening. She was fine—so we carried on just feeding in the evenings and the mornings."
>
> *Farida, mother of Olivia, 2*

Although you may be at work all day, you'll probably want to make sure that your baby eats at least some of his meals with you. If your baby is going to be cared for by someone else from the very start of BLW and you don't want to miss out on any of his early experiments with food, you could try sharing breakfast and an evening meal with him, and letting him have just milk feedings during the day for the first week or so, until you

BREAST-FEEDING WHEN YOU GO
BACK TO WORK

Some mothers express their breast milk so it can be given to their baby while they're at work; others find it easier if their baby has formula when he's with his babysitter. Your decision will probably depend on factors such as how many hours a day you will be apart from your baby and how supportive your boss and colleagues are. Many mothers find that breast-feeding morning and evening when they go back to work is a good way to reconnect with their baby when they have to be out all day.

Remember that while your baby is under a year old he should still be having plenty of milk feedings. Some babies are happy to go without a milk feeding during the day and catch up with their breast milk intake when they are back with their mother. Many mothers are surprised by just how adaptable their babies are and how flexible breast-feeding is. However, if you will be away from your baby for long periods and you don't want to leave expressed breast milk for him it is probably better to provide some formula for his caregiver to offer him, rather than expect him to suddenly eat more solid food.

For specific advice on breast-feeding and working, talk to your pediatrician, a local breast-feeding counselor, or a voluntary helpline.

feel ready to let your child care provider offer him food. He won't need to be on three meals a day for a few months, and he won't go hungry as long as you don't drop any milk feedings.

Some parents may be anxious to get their baby "on to solids" before they go back to work and may be tempted to start earlier than six months, or to cut down on milk feedings quickly. This isn't a good idea—and it's unlikely to succeed if you're following BLW. If your baby isn't ready he simply won't take an interest in food and, if you try to persuade him, he'll probably start to dislike the whole idea.

If your baby's caregiver doesn't want to do BLW you may have to reach a compromise. Babies are very adaptable and, while he may find it confusing at first that things aren't the same when he's with someone else, your little one will quickly learn to expect different things from different people. The most important thing is that your baby's caregiver should respect your views about allowing him to "say" when he's had enough. If they regularly encourage him to eat more than he needs he may start to cut down his milk feedings too early and become reliant on puréed foods to satisfy his hunger. This could lead to his being frustrated during BLW meals at home. However, it's unlikely to be more than a month or two before your babysitter feels confident to let your baby handle food himself.

7.

A Healthy Diet for Everyone

"Baby-led weaning provides a great opportunity to discuss what the whole family eats. Wanting to make sure their baby gets the best gives a lot of parents the push they need to make changes in their own diet."

Elizabeth, public health nurse

"They know when they're having the same food as you and when they're not. And you're very aware that they know this. So if you're having ice cream with sprinkles on the top, that's what the baby's having as well. So it makes you think about what you eat."

Mary, mother of Elsie, 23 months

The Importance of Healthy Eating

Eating normal family food and being included in mealtimes are at the heart of BLW, and many parents use the introduction of solids to make sure the whole family is eating well. Getting your baby used to having nutritious family food every day will give her the best chance of making healthy choices throughout her life.

This chapter isn't intended as an in-depth guide to infant nutrition; it's a basic guide to healthy eating for the whole family. Babies learn by copying, so if everyone in the family is eating a good diet your baby will want to do the same. The kind of food your baby learns to expect is completely up to you—she isn't yet under any pressure from advertising or friends to eat badly, and she's too young to go shopping by herself!

Making an effort to have a healthy diet doesn't mean worrying about your baby's nutrition or trying to control what she eats. As long as you're offering her a balanced diet you can rely on her to take what she needs when she needs it. Remember that for the first few months of solids very little of her nutrition will come from family food anyway— breast milk or formula will supply almost all the nutrients she needs. She's still learning about tastes, textures, and managing food, but it's important that the food she is offered is healthy and varied, so that the extra nutrients she *does* need are readily available to her.

As your baby gets older you may find that she goes through phases of wanting a particular food and nothing else, even if you offer her perfectly balanced meals every day. For example, she may "binge" on carbohydrates for a few days, or have a day when all she wants to eat is meat. However eccentric her choice of food seems, this is normal behavior for babies and toddlers (see page 146). So there's no need to worry too much about what your child eats at each meal or snack as long as you *offer* her something from each of the main food groups each day (see page 185).

Much of the information in this chapter relates to adults and older children, to help you to provide healthy meals for all ages. However, there are a couple of important points to bear in mind when preparing a meal that your baby will share:

- Babies need more fat than adults and less fiber (see pages 193 and 194).
- There are some foods that should babies shouldn't have (see pages 96–101).

If you feel your family's diet may be lacking specific nutrients, check the grid on pages 198 and 199 to see which common foods contain the vitamins and minerals that are especially important for babies.

BLW STORY

I have a terrible relationship with food that I don't want my daughter Elinor to repeat. I hope that if she is in control of what she eats from the start, then the dinner table won't become a battleground for her the way it was for me.

As a toddler I had to sit at the table until I had finished all my food and I often used to gag and vomit the food back up. But it was a power struggle I always won because no one can really make you eat. Even now I eat "like a child" and gag on lots of flavors and textures.

To be honest, as Elinor approached six months, the thought of having to cook (and taste) those awful-smelling purées was really making me dread starting solids with her. If I didn't want to eat them, why on earth would she? My nurse was great—she was really happy when I mentioned BLW. I later found out she had done something similar with her own children, years ago.

And now that I have to set a good example with food it's actually forcing me to eat better myself. I used to just eat things like canned spaghetti, but now I want Elinor to see me eating healthy foods. There's more healthy stuff in the fridge nowadays and it's having a really positive impact on our diet.

Jackie, mother of Elinor, 7 months

Knowing the Basics

So how do you make sure your family has a healthy, balanced diet? It's probably not as difficult as it may seem at first. Most traditional meals from cultures around the world are fairly well balanced, and a varied diet based on fresh foods with plenty of fruit and vegetables will almost certainly provide your baby and the rest of the family with all the essential nutrients. However, once you include fast foods, prepackaged meals, and processed snacks in your diet, the balance can easily tip toward too much saturated fat, salt, and sugar, and not enough vitamins and minerals. A diet like this is linked to the development of heart disease, diabetes, and cancer in later life, and salty foods are especially dangerous for babies.

A balanced diet is one that has all the nutrients needed for health and that is based on the main food groups in the right proportions. Fruit, vegetables, grains, and carbohydrates should form the bulk of your family's diet, with small amounts of protein- and calcium-rich foods and a little healthy fat or oil. The following is roughly the balance of portions per day that adults and older children should aim for (a portion is roughly the amount each person can hold in one open hand):

- vegetables and fruit: five (three of vegetables and two of fruit is ideal)
- grains and starchy vegetables (rice, potatoes, pasta, bread, etc.): two to three
- meat, fish, and other protein-rich foods such as lentils: one
- cheese, milk, yogurt, and other calcium-rich foods such as hummus and small-boned fish (e.g., sardines): one
- healthy fats (such as olive oil, nuts, and seeds): a quarter of a portion

While babies will tend to eat proportionately more protein and fats than adults, and toddlers will often eat larger amounts of carbohydrates, it's still useful to bear in mind that a baby-sized portion is a baby-sized handful. This is much less than many people expect babies to eat. Remember too that you shouldn't expect your baby to be getting all her nourishment from solid foods until she's about a year, so the handful "rule" won't really be a true guide until then.

> "A bonus effect of BLW for some of the families that I've worked with was that they actually started to make improvements to their own diets as a result of preparing fresh, nutritious foods for their babies, learning new cooking skills, and developing an interest in their family's health."
>
> *Julie, nutritionist*

Variety is the Spice of Life!

Along with keeping an eye on the balance of foods, making sure your baby is offered a *varied* diet is probably one of the most important things you can do to ensure good nutrition. A varied diet is more likely to include foods from all the different groups, providing your baby with a broad range of vitamins and minerals. A limited diet—however healthy it may be—restricts the chances of your baby getting everything she needs. Exposing her to a broad range of foods will also give your baby a better chance to experience different tastes, smells, and textures, making her more open to new foods when she's older.

If your shopping list is roughly the same each week it may be a good idea to start including some new foods. Think about any habits you may have developed with food—many people eat the same thing for breakfast every day or have a small range of favorite dishes that they eat every week. A diet like this may not be unhealthy, but it won't offer your baby much variety. If she doesn't like all the foods *you* like, then her options may be severely limited as she grows up.

Try the following tips to ensure variety.

Fruit and vegetables

- Aim for as many fruit and vegetables as possible with different-colored flesh: red, yellow, green, orange, and purple—they each contain different nutrients.
- Try out a few fruits and vegetables you don't normally buy.
- Think about using fresh herbs, such as parsley, cilantro, and basil—they contain a good range of vitamins and minerals.

Grains and starches (carbohydrates)

- If you normally have potatoes as your main carbohydrate, try using rice or other grains now and then (or vice versa).
- Root vegetables, such as sweet potatoes, can often be used in place of ordinary potatoes.
- Millet, bulgar, couscous, or quinoa can all be used in place of rice in many dishes, and more and more supermarkets are stocking them.
- Be adventurous! Alternate your usual breakfast cereal with cereals made from a different grain.
- Buckwheat or spelt flour can be used in place of ordinary wheat in baking or cooking.
- Rye or pumpernickel bread, or one of the other nonwheat breads, can be substituted for "normal" bread now and again.
- If you normally eat pasta or noodles made from wheat, why not try a nonwheat version for a change?

Protein-rich foods

- Not all cuts of meat have the same nutrients—chicken legs have different nutrients from the breast, for example.
- Liver is usually full of nutrients (organic versions are best as they contain fewer toxins).
- Chicken, beef, lamb, and pork are all good meat choices, but game and fowl such as venison, partridge, rabbit, duck, and goose are also nutritious (though they do tend to be expensive).
- Beans, lentils, and split peas, have different nutrients from animal-based proteins, and they're great for nonvegetarians, too. Try adding them to casseroles or curries.

Calcium-rich foods

- You don't have to stick to dairy products every day to get enough calcium—sardines and hummus are also good sources.
- Be adventurous with cheese. There are many different varieties made from cows' milk—and, of course, from sheep's milk and goats' milk, too.
- Some bread is fortified with calcium.

Junk Food

Commercially prepared foods that contain high levels of sugar, salt, or saturated fats (cakes, chocolate, cookies, chips, pastry, and pies) aren't really necessary at all and should be eaten in moderation only—preferably a couple of times a week at most.

Those containing high levels of salt, trans-fatty acids, or hydro-genated fats are best avoided completely.

Of course, this doesn't mean that you should *never* give your baby commercially made cakes or cookies, but bear in mind that they are not the best foods, nutritionally speaking. And you can make far more nutritious versions at home by sweet-ening cakes or cookies with banana or dried fruit, adding oats to cookies, or simply using a smaller amount of sugar than the recipe suggests—and your baby or toddler will enjoy helping you to make them, too.

It's probably realistic to apply the 80/20 rule: if you make sure at least 80 percent of your child's diet is really nutritious, then you can afford to risk the odd "bad" food without doing her any harm. Banning these foods (especially when your child can see others eating them) *or* using them as treats or rewards for good behavior will just make them more desirable (see page 171). If *you* don't eat them every day, then your child won't expect to, either.

Vegetarians and Vegans

Diets that exclude certain foods risk being low in some nutri-ents. A vegetarian diet may be low in iron and protein, while a vegan diet (where no meat, fish, eggs, or dairy products are eaten) may lack B vitamins, iron, zinc, calcium, and some amino acids. Parents who are planning to bring up their baby as a vegan will need to be particularly careful to ensure she gets sufficient nutrients.

Beans, lentils, and peas, dried fruits such as apricots, figs, and prunes, and green leafy vegetables are good sources of iron. Vitamin C helps with absorption of iron, so eating fruits and vegetables that are high in vitamin C (or drinking diluted, freshly squeezed juice) with meals will help to ensure that the maximum amount of the iron available in the food is absorbed.

Vegetarians can get good amounts of protein from dairy foods, but using cheese as the main protein source at every meal is not recommended because of its relatively high fat and salt content. Very few nonanimal proteins contain all the essential amino acids, but combining certain foods can help to compensate for this.

If, as a family, you have a diet that leaves out a number of foods, you may wish to discuss what you are planning to offer your baby with a dietitian or nutritionist, who will advise you on how to choose healthy food combinations and tell you if supplements are needed for your baby.

Getting the Best Out of the Food You Buy

The demand for cheap foods with a long shelf life means that most foods in the developed world contain chemicals: crops are often sprayed with pesticides or fungicides, and artificial flavorings, preservatives, and colors are commonly added when processed foods are made. Many of these chemicals are potentially harmful, and there is little research into their combined effects on babies and children. Unfortunately foods that are produced organically and *don't* contain any chemicals tend to be expensive. When it comes to organic it doesn't need to be "all or nothing." Even if you can't afford (or can't find) totally organic foods you can still minimize the amount of undesirable chemicals in the food you buy, and there are plenty of ways to make sure you get as many nutrients as possible from your food, whether it's organic or not:

- Go for organic foods if you can afford them, perhaps prioritizing the foods your child eats most often (in particular, nonorganic meat, eggs, root vegetables, and small grains such as wheat usually contain much higher levels of chemicals than organic varieties). And compare prices—some organic foods, such as milk, aren't much more expensive than nonorganic.
- Check out your local organic food delivery service; they are often cheaper than store-bought organics—and they may even save you money because you won't be tempted to buy unnecessary "extras," as you would in the supermarket.
- Buy locally grown fruit or vegetables that are in season— they will be fresher than imported produce. (Imported foods have not only been stored for longer but are also likely to have been harvested before they are really ripe, which is also before all the vitamins have fully developed.)
- If buying organic, eat fruit and vegetables with the peel on where possible—many of the nutrients are just under the skin. (The skin of nonorganic varieties tends to contain pesticides, so you may prefer to peel them.)
- Wash all nonorganic fruit and vegetables (including salad vegetables) with a little diluted vinegar or commercial "veggi wash" to remove superficial waxes and pesticides.
- Steam vegetables rather than boiling them, to reduce nutrient loss.
- Use any water from cooking vegetables for sauces or gravy, so the nutrients aren't wasted.
- Wherever possible, cut up fruit and vegetables just before eating/cooking them; alternatively, cover and refrigerate them. (Some of the food's vitamin C is lost from cut surfaces, especially at room temperature.)
- Serve food as soon as possible after cooking.

- If you need an alternative to fresh vegetables choose frozen rather than canned or dried versions—they generally contain more vitamins.
- If you *do* buy canned foods, choose varieties in their own juice, plain water, or oil, not in syrup or salted water (brine). Look for brands of baked beans that are low in salt and sugar.
- Avoid prepackaged meals as much as you can.

A Basic Guide to Nutrients

We all need a range of nutrients to help keep our bodies healthy. Below is a brief outline of the main categories of nutrients that all humans need to obtain through their food. Your baby's milk feedings contain all these in the proportions she needs for the first six months of her life. By the time she's about one year old she'll be able to get all of them from other foods.

Vitamins and minerals

These are needed for overall health. They are involved in the functioning of most of the body's systems and for ensuring a healthy immune system. Fruit and vegetables provide many of the vitamins and minerals we need, but a few are obtained more easily from grains or animal products.

Carbohydrates

Carbohydrates are used mainly for energy. They come in two digestible forms: sugar and starch. Sugar provides an immediate "rush," whereas starch is broken down gradually and provides more "slow-release" energy. Fruits are a good source of naturally occurring sugar—much better for babies and adults than the "empty calories" provided by the sort of sugar that is added to drinks and sweets. Most foods contain at least some carbohydrate; whole grains and vegetables such as potatoes are particularly good for prolonged energy.

Proteins

These are needed mainly for growth and repair of body tissues. Adult bodies contain a large amount of protein in their muscles and organs, all of which has to be replenished as it wears out. Children need proportionately more protein than their parents because their bodies are growing.

Proteins are made up of building blocks called amino acids, but not all protein foods contain all the amino acids we need. In general, animal proteins are "complete" proteins while proteins from legumes (such as beans and lentils), mycoproteins (such as Quorn), and grains (such as rice and wheat) are "partial" proteins. Eating grains with legumes or mycoproteins (not necessarily at the same meal) provides the equivalent of a complete protein. The only nonanimal proteins that contain all the essential amino acids are the soybean (in the form of TVP, tempeh, tofu, or soy milk) and quinoa (a South American grain similar to couscous in appearance, with a light, nutty flavor—a useful alternative to rice).

Fats

Fats are needed for the healthy functioning of the brain and nerves. They are also a useful source of energy. Because they are concentrated, only small quantities are needed. There are two types of fat: saturated and unsaturated. Saturated fats come mostly from animal sources and, on their own, they tend to be solid at room temperature (for example, butter and lard). Unsaturated fats are usually found in vegetables, nuts, and seeds but are also present in oily fish. Unsaturated fats are generally better for health, although saturated fats are not as bad for young children as they are for adults.

Babies need more fat in their diet than adults. The best fats for your baby (and for adults) are the essential fatty acids (Omega-3 and Omega-6) and monounsaturated oils. Omega-3 is especially good for brain development; it is found in fish oils and, more recently, is added to some pastas and juices—but the best source is breast milk!

Fiber

Strictly speaking, fiber isn't a nutrient, but it is important to include it in our diets because it provides roughage, which helps to prevent constipation and ensure a healthy bowel. It also makes us feel full for longer. There are two types of fiber: insoluble and soluble. Insoluble fiber is found in whole-wheat products (such as whole-wheat bread and pasta), and wheat bran. Soluble fiber is found in oats, fruit, peas, lentils, chick-peas, and brown rice.

Although both types of fiber are good for adults and older children, too much insoluble fiber can irritate a baby's digestive tract, and when it is in a very concentrated form (as in raw bran) it can also inhibit the absorption of minerals such as calcium and iron. Very high-fiber foods such as bran-based cereals shouldn't be given to young children.

Whole-wheat foods contain a lot of fiber, which means we need to eat a lot of them to get enough nutrients from them. Babies haven't got enough room in their tummies to do this, and there is a risk that they will lack nutrients if they eat too much of this type of food. Making sure you offer other nutritious foods when giving your baby whole-wheat bread or pasta will allow her to limit the amount of insoluble fiber she eats, naturally.

Babies do, however, need plenty of *soluble* fiber for a healthy bowel system and bulky stools—so there is no need to limit the amount of foods such as oats, lentils, brown rice, peas, and fruit in your child's diet.

NUTS

Nuts are very nutritious; they are a good source of protein and energy because they are high in fat. However, nuts are hard to bite and chew and, if they should get into the airway, don't soften and dissolve like most other foods. *They therefore present a serious choking risk to young children.* Nuts, especially peanuts, are also commonly associated with allergy. If you have a family history of nut allergies, and even if you don't, you will probably want to avoid giving your baby nut products, such as peanut butter, until she is at least two years old, and quite possibly for longer (you may want to check with your pediatrician first). It's generally recommended that children should not be allowed to eat whole nuts until they are over three years old.

Good sources at a glance

The grid on pages 198–199 shows the common sources of nutrients that are especially important to babies. A healthy, balanced diet is easily achieved by eating some of each of the nutrients every day. The better the food as a source of that nutrient, the more check marks we've given it in the grid. Where there is no check mark, the food may still contain traces of the nutrient but the amount is not enough to be significant.

Some nutrients (for example vitamin E and selenium) are quite difficult to avoid, so we haven't included these in the grid. We have, however, picked out **vitamins A**, **B**, **C**, and **D**, **iron** (needed for healthy blood), and **calcium** (for healthy bones) for a special mention as some diets can be short of these. Zinc is an important mineral that can be low in many diets. However, because it tends to be found in many of the same foods as iron, we haven't listed it separately.

As you'll see, many single foods have lots of different nutrients. So a dish such as grilled salmon or mackerel with rice, peas, and carrots will provide carbohydrate, protein, iron, calcium, healthy fats, and many vitamins and minerals. A piece of fruit for dessert will top it off nicely.

Did You Know?

- Olive oil is good for cooking—the darker it is, the better it is for you.
- Although oily fish is one of the most nutritious foods around, current guidelines suggest that babies, toddlers, and pregnant women should have no more than two portions of oily fish (such as sardines) a week, because of worries that low levels of mercury could be potentially harmful.
- Fresh tuna counts as an oily fish and contains good quantities of the essential fatty acid Omega-3; canned tuna has much less because the canning process reduces the level of Omega-3s. As noted above, it's best to limit your baby's

intake of canned tuna to no more than two portions a week (or one portion of albacore tuna a week, as this is higher in mercury).

- Shark, swordfish, mackerel, and marlin contain high levels of pollutants (mainly because they feed on other fish), so they are best avoided.
- Eating a whole fruit is better for you than drinking the juice alone—not only because it contains more roughage this way but also because you get more vitamin C.
- Avocados contain quite a lot of healthy fat, so they're more "filling" than most other fruits.
- Soy contains high levels of aluminum and plant estrogens, so soy products, such as soy milk and textured vegetable protein (TVP), shouldn't be eaten too frequently (especially by babies).
- Liver is a very good source of nutrients, especially iron, but it shouldn't normally be eaten more than once or twice a week because it contains very high levels of vitamin A, which can be toxic in large quantities. It is also the organ that deals with the waste products for the animal while it is alive, so it may contain concentrated levels of some chemicals and other pollutants, although this can be minimized by choosing organically produced liver.
- Spinach is not as good a source of iron as Popeye would have us believe! This is because it also contains phytates, which actually interfere with the absorption of iron.
- Tea contains phytates, too, which is why it is best drunk separately from meals and is not recommended for young children.

Nutrient → / Type of food ↓	Vitamin A / betacarotene	B group vitamins
citrus fruits, e.g. orange, grapefruit, satsuma		
berries and currants, kiwi		
apricots, figs, prunes		
bananas		✓✓
other fruits, peppers	✓ (orange and yellow	
green leafy vegetables	✓	
root vegetables, e.g., carrots, parsnips	✓ (orange and yellow)	
starchy vegetables, e.g., potatoes, yams		✓
legumes, e.g., chickpeas, baked beans, peas, lentils		
soy beans and soy products (including TVP and tofu)		✓✓✓
cereals/grains, (including bread and pasta) e.g., wheat, couscous, buckwheat, rice, barley, millet, quinoa**, oats		✓✓✓
red meat, e.g., beef, lamb		✓✓✓
liver	✓✓✓	✓✓✓
white meat and poultry, e.g., chicken, duck, pork		✓✓✓
oily fish, e.g., mackerel, sardine, salmon	✓✓✓	✓✓
other fish, e.g., plaice, cod, sole	✓	✓✓
eggs	✓✓✓	✓✓✓
milk, yogurt	✓✓	✓
butter, cream, margarine	✓	✓
cheese	✓✓	✓✓
fresh (finely ground) nuts, e.g., walnut, almond, brazil		
vegetable, nut and seed oils, e.g., olive oil, walnut oil, sesame seed oil		

* These are the healthiest fats for the whole family; other types of fat are good for your baby, because they are a concentrated source of energy, but less good for everyone else because too much of them contributes to heart disease.

Vitamin C	Vitamin D / calcium	Iron	Carbohydrate	Protein	Fat *	Fiber
✓✓✓			✓✓			✓✓
✓✓✓			✓✓			✓✓
✓✓		✓✓	✓✓			✓✓✓
✓✓			✓✓✓			✓✓✓
✓✓			✓✓	✓ (avocado)	✓ (avocado)*	✓✓
✓✓	✓	✓✓				✓✓
✓			✓✓			✓✓
✓			✓✓✓			✓
✓		✓✓	✓✓	✓✓✓ (partial)	✓*	✓✓
	✓	✓		✓✓✓	✓*	✓✓
		✓ (whole grains)	✓✓✓	✓✓✓ (partial)**		✓✓✓***
		✓✓✓		✓✓✓	✓✓	
	✓✓	✓✓✓		✓✓✓		
		✓✓		✓✓✓	✓✓	
✓✓✓				✓✓✓	✓✓*	
✓				✓✓✓	✓	
✓✓✓	✓			✓✓✓	✓	
✓✓			✓	✓	✓✓	
✓✓					✓✓✓	
✓✓✓			✓	✓✓	✓✓	
		✓✓	✓✓		✓✓*	✓
					✓✓✓*	

** Quinoa is considered a complete source of protein.
*** Whole-grains and whole-grain cereals (e.g. whole wheat bread and pasta and brown rice) contain large amounts of insoluble fiber, so babies shouldn't have them at every meal.

8.

Troubleshooting

Once BLW is under way you may find you have all sorts of queries and concerns about how your baby is managing food. This chapter aims to answer the most frequently asked questions, from concerns about starting BLW to why your 10-month-old throws food from his high chair and what you can do about it. Of course, all babies are different, so although most of the questions are arranged in order of age, most of the answers can be applied to babies at any stage of BLW.

Is there any harm in doing a bit of BLW and a bit of spoon-feeding?

Most babies find it more fun to feed themselves than to be fed by someone else—they enjoy doing things for themselves and learning new skills. Many parents have turned to BLW because their baby already refuses to be spoon-fed.

There is a myth that babies must be persuaded to accept spoon-feeding. These are some of the common reasons why people believe that spoon-feeding is necessary:

- A mistaken belief that babies have to "get used to a spoon" by a certain age.
- A mistaken belief that babies need to have yogurt every day and that they won't be able to eat it by themselves.
- Worries about the mess there will be if the baby feeds himself runny foods.
- Concerns that the baby isn't eating enough on his own and that he needs to be "topped off" with some puréed food.

Some parents want their baby to be used to being spoon-fed in case they ever need to do it, and some simply want to have the option to spoon-feed alongside finger foods.

However, your baby may have other ideas! Many BLW babies quickly make it clear that they don't want to be fed by someone else. There are all kinds of ways they do this—most commonly simply by taking the spoon from the other person's hand. This seems to be especially true of breast-fed babies, who are used to being in control of their own feeding. Bear in mind that if you sometimes insist on spoon-feeding your child, while letting him feed himself at other times, he will be getting mixed messages about how much you trust him and how independent he is allowed to be.

If your baby does accept a spoon, there's no harm in combining spoon-feeding with self-feeding. However, if you are attracted to BLW because of its advantages for your baby (see page 20), we recommend that you don't spoon-feed at every meal. This is because, if you do, your baby may not get enough variety of texture, or as many opportunities as he could to develop his skills. There's also a chance you might be tempted to persuade him to eat more than he wants. It's better to reserve spoon-feeding for certain foods (yogurt or cereal, for example) or to hand your baby a spoon ready-loaded with food every now and then and let him decide whether or not to eat it. (See page 113 for tips on how to make runny foods easier for your baby to manage on his own.)

> "I try to spoon-feed Sammy when we are out so it's less messy, but he's not happy with it. He doesn't make a fuss, but he usually just spits the food out, looks at it, then picks it up and eats it from his fingers."
>
> *Claire, mother of Sammy, 10 months*

> "When we have things like cereal I sometimes feed Nicholas—but it's when he wants me to; I'm not trying to force it. And when he doesn't want it any more, I stop." *Dan, father of William, 3, and Nicholas, 7 months*

My daughter used to stuff her mouth full of food when she started to feed herself at nine months. I'm frightened to let my six-month-old son feed himself in case he does the same thing.

Older babies overstuffing their mouths with food is something that seems to be less of a problem with BLW than with the conventional method of introducing solids. It's possible that babies who are allowed to explore food from the start learn not to overfill their mouths because they have been trained by the gag reflex, which is triggered quite far forward on the tongue when a baby is young (see page 46). It seems likely that babies who are allowed to take food to their mouths as soon as they can will be less, not more, likely to overfill their mouths.

What you can do:

- Let your baby experiment with food from six months.
- Make sure he is sitting upright.

- Try not to distract him while he is eating—let him concentrate.
- If he gags, don't panic—this reflex will help him to learn how much is too much.

It sounds as though BLW will involve a lot of food being wasted. We're on a tight budget and can't afford to throw food away. How can we avoid too much waste?

This is a common concern for parents thinking about doing BLW. There is always some waste when babies start on solids—even with purées—and BLW may be less wasteful than spoon-feeding and may even work out to be cheaper. This is because:

- Baby-led weaning babies eat pretty much the same foods as their parents; buying a few extra vegetables (for example) will make much less difference to the overall weekly food bill than stocking up on commercial baby foods.
- Puréeing your own food at home can be very wasteful— lots of food gets left in sieves and blenders.
- Some food will end up on the high chair or the floor however you feed your baby; pieces of food are easier to pick up and hand back for another round than dollops of purée.
- Babies who are allowed to feed themselves from the beginning of weaning seem to be less likely to be picky eaters later; picky eaters waste a lot of food.
- Finally, if you have a dog you may even be able to cut back on dog food; dogs quickly learn to patrol the area around a baby who is self-feeding!

Here are some tips for keeping waste to a minimum:

- Plan ahead to make sure any food that gets thrown or dropped lands on a clean surface, such as a table cloth or splash mat, so that it can be handed back to your baby (or eaten by you).
- Make all your meals something that your baby can share (this should be easy as long as your diet is fairly healthy, see Chapter 7).
- Give your baby only a few pieces of food to play with at once; if you overload him he's likely to want to "clear the decks" just so he can concentrate.
- Be as relaxed as you can while your baby is learning how to manage food, and let him take his time. The amount he wastes will soon get less as his skills develop.
- Resist the temptation to encourage your baby to "eat up." Making him eat more than he needs may mean he leaves less but it may interfere with his feelings of fullness and lead to his gaining more weight than he should—so it isn't really any less wasteful.

My baby is seven months old, and I feel I don't know how much he should be eating or how many different foods I should be giving him. I keep going back to the food he likes just to make sure he eats something.

A healthy baby of seven months doesn't really need much more than breast milk or formula; at this age solid food is all about exploring, learning, and practicing skills. But letting go of some of the old ideas about having to get food into a baby is hard for many parents, and trusting their baby to eat what he needs can be difficult. Babies vary a great deal in how fast they get going with solid foods; at seven months many babies have barely started.

At first BLW babies often eat smaller quantities than their parents expect they will—especially compared to the quantities of food that some purée-fed babies are able to put away. But building up solids gradually and keeping plenty of milk feedings in the early days is far better for your baby than rushing him to increase his solids (see page 141).

So there's no need to limit the foods you offer your baby to food you know he likes just to make sure he eats something. At seven months he's still learning that food is fun and that it tastes nice, so it's better to give him the chance to try lots of different tastes. (This will also maximize the range of nutrients he has—even if he doesn't eat much.) It's also important to give him the opportunity to practice with different shapes and textures, rather than to limit him to foods he can manage easily, so that he can develop his self-feeding skills. But he doesn't need to have an enormous range of foods at every mealtime. (In fact, he may get a bit overwhelmed if you put too much in front of him at once, see page 71.)

Parents often assume that their baby doesn't like a particular food if he spits it out or rejects it when it's offered—but it may simply be that he doesn't feel like it that day, or that he doesn't need it. Babies and small children are notoriously fickle in their tastes—they'll eat lots of something one day and then not want it the next. This is normal. Just keep offering foods that you usually eat and make sure there's variety. And try not to talk about foods as his "favorites" or ones he doesn't like. Babies tend to act in the way they think their parents expect them to, so if you keep saying he doesn't like a particular food he'll end up believing you!

If your baby is formula-fed, he may be slower to accept lots of new tastes in the early days of solids because, up until now, all his feedings have tasted the same. Although it may take longer for formula-fed babies to try new things, it's still important to offer them a variety of foods so they can broaden their range when they are ready.

The best approach is to give your baby some of what you're eating (as long as it's nutritious), so that he feels included in the meal and knows that the food is safe (see page 21). Then sit back and let him do what he wants with it. If he doesn't want to eat it, then he doesn't need to—there's no need to empty the fridge looking for something to tempt him.

What you can do:

- Keep offering foods that are normally on the family menu.
- Remember that milk feedings are still enough to nourish your baby.
- Offer a variety of tastes.
- Offer a variety of shapes and textures.
- Don't put too much on your baby's plate (or high chair tray).
- Eat the same food as your baby whenever possible.
- Expect your baby's likes and dislikes to change from day to day and week to week.
- Trust him if he doesn't want to eat.

People keep asking me how much he's having, but I can't really tell because it ends up all over him!

Health professionals, relatives, and friends tend to ask, "How much is he having?" and they expect parents to say, "Three spoonfuls twice a day," or "Two whole jars three times a day." But BLW is about variety, tastes, textures, and learning, not about the amounts and quantities that most people are familiar with from spoon-feeding.

When babies feed themselves it can be very difficult, at first, to tell how much they have eaten. Once the baby has spread the food around his high chair tray, lost some under his bottom, and dropped bits onto the floor, working out what must have been swallowed is a real challenge. And when we are giving babies sticks of food to hold we aren't measuring it in teaspoonfuls in the first place. And yet, although we understand all this, we still want to know "how much."

But most people's ideas about the amounts babies "should" eat are not realistic (see page 141). They are often a relic from the days when every mother wanted to produce the fattest baby around. "Chubby" equaled "healthy," and a large weight gain was the goal to aim for. So the more the baby ate, the better.

Our ideas about amounts are also based on puréed food. But when food is puréed, water is usually added to make it the right consistency, so what looks like a lot of food may in fact contain very little solid stuff. And bear in mind that, although a spoon-fed baby may get through a whole jar, he, too, will be covered in quite a lot of it.

The truth is it doesn't matter how much your child is eating as long as he is healthy, has plenty of opportunities to eat as much as he needs, and is having as many milk feedings as he wants.

What you can do:

- Try not to feel under pressure to gauge how much your baby is eating. As long as he is offered a variety of nutritious foods and is still having plenty of milk feedings, it doesn't matter.
- When people ask "How much is he eating?", list all the different foods he has tried, and talk about how much he enjoys eating, rather than be drawn into estimating quantities.

"My grandma asked me the other day how much Leo was having. I said, 'Oh, he's having loads! Carrot, broccoli, chicken, banana, avocado, beans, toast, olives, cheese—everything.' She didn't know what to say!"

Claire, mother of Leo, 8 months

My baby is eight months old and we have been doing well with BLW. The only problem is that his weight gain has slowed down. What's happening?

Babies' growth rates vary enormously—both from baby to baby and for each baby individually. However, many parents who have followed BLW report a period of slow weight gain at around eight months. This seems to happen just before their baby begins to eat significant amounts of food, when the weight gain speeds up again.

The growth charts used by doctors show the range of weights that is normal at different ages; when your baby is weighed his progress is plotted as dots, which are joined up to make a line. But very few babies get steadily heavier week by week; they tend to do it in spurts, so the chances are the line will be staggered or have plateaus when nothing happens for a few weeks. This is normal (and it's one good reason why, for babies over six to eight weeks, weighing more than once a month is not usually helpful). The curved lines on the chart are a generalized guide to help health professionals spot babies who really aren't growing as they should; they don't mean that any one baby is expected to follow one line. However, if your baby appears well but hasn't gained any weight for several weeks, it's reasonable to have a chat with your pediatrician and maybe have him check your baby over—just to confirm there's nothing wrong.

In general, breast-fed babies have a similar growth pattern to one another: they grow rapidly for the first three months and then begin to slow down as they approach six months. This continues until they are about nine months old, when they settle into a steadier rate of growth. Formula-fed babies tend to grow less fast at first but faster later (however, it is now recognized that, ideally, they, too, should follow the breast-fed pattern).

Not *all* weight gain is good for babies and children. Indeed, excessive weight gain can be at least as harmful to health as inadequate gain—both in childhood and in later life. If your baby has been growing faster than average until now, a period of less rapid growth may be what he needs to even things up.

Bear in mind that even if your baby is putting on very little weight he will continue to grow (in length) and develop. When babies eat and drink, all the nutrients and calories they take in go first to making sure their brain and other organs are able to function and grow and then to providing them with energy to move around. Any spare calories are stored as extra weight. So a baby who is not putting on much weight probably has enough food for health and growth, but simply has very little to spare. Lack of weight gain doesn't mean he is starving.

What you can do:

- Look at your child as a whole. If he seems well and active there is probably nothing to worry about.
- Look at the overall pattern of your baby's weight, not just the last few weeks: actual weight *loss* is a cause for concern but a short period of slow weight gain alone is rarely significant.
- Discuss your child's weight with your pediatrician if you are worried.

My eight-month-old often strains to do a bowel movement—why is this?

Babies often make a real song and dance about having a bowel movement, even when it's quite soft. It's not clear why this is, but it doesn't seem to be related to what or how they eat. One theory says that straining starts to happen when the baby discovers that he can actually control this process—and that he may even get some enjoyment out of it! Whatever the truth, it seems that most babies will do it at some time.

However, if your baby's stool is really hard, this suggests that he is not having enough fluid in his diet. Constipation like this is very unlikely to happen if he is breast-fed, especially if all his drinks are breast-feeds, because breast milk has a natural laxative effect that keeps everything moving at a steady pace. If you are formula-feeding, it may be that you need to offer your baby more frequent drinks of water. Just occasionally, a hard stool is a symptom of an underlying illness, so it doesn't hurt to get your baby checked by a doctor if the problem persists. (See also page 139.)

What you can do:

- Offer frequent breast-feeds, or drinks of water if he is formula-fed.
- If hard stools continue have your baby checked by a doctor.

My baby's stool is really runny. Is this normal?

Stools that are very loose or runny are fairly common during weaning, whether or not the process is baby-led. It's just a feature of your baby's digestive system getting used to other foods; they will change to being firmer over time. If your baby is breast-fed, his stool has probably always been soft, and it may stay like this for several months, especially if all his drinks are of breast milk.

When babies' stool is runnier than normal they often want to drink a lot. If you are breast-feeding, that means continuing to feed your baby whenever he wants. If you are formula-feeding, offer your baby frequent drinks of water—but don't be worried if he turns them down; that's just his way of saying, "No thanks, I'm fine."

Sometimes runny stool is a sign that a baby is not able to digest certain foods or that he has an infection. If your baby is not thriving or seems unwell in any way, you should have him checked by a doctor; runny stools on their own are normal but with other signs, such as vomiting, listlessness or weight loss, they may not be. (See also page 140.)

What you can do:

- Offer your baby frequent breast-feeds, or drinks of water if he is formula-fed.
- Use a barrier cream to prevent diaper rash and change his diaper as soon as he's dirty (very runny stool can make a baby's bottom sore).
- Keep an eye open for any signs of illness and get him checked by a doctor if you think he could be unwell.

My baby doesn't seem to have eaten anything for a couple of days. He's nine months. What should I do?

If your baby is off his food for a couple of days, it's probably nothing to worry about. It is not at all unusual for babies to eat very little for several meals—and then to eat everything in sight for a day or so (see page 146). Sometimes the reason is as simple as something like teething: it may hurt him to eat solid food and he may need the comfort of breast or bottle (breast-feeding is especially good for easing teething pain). Babies also tend to eat less and drink more when they have a cold or other minor infection. This is natural; digesting food takes considerable energy and not eating gives the baby a chance to use all his energy to fight the infection. Once the cold has gone, everything will get back to normal. A baby who has a more serious illness may also lose his appetite, but you'll notice other symptoms, too. So if your baby loses his appetite *and* is pale, listless, or crying a lot, or has other signs of illness, you should get him checked by a doctor.

Emotional issues can sometimes turn a baby off food—babies can stop eating solids for a day or two when their mother goes back to work after maternity leave, or if they change day care, nanny, or babysitter. Sometimes stress in the parents' relationship or big changes such as moving to a new house (or even going on vacation) can affect a baby's appetite. And there are some babies who regularly skip food for a couple of days (and then eat lots for a few days) for no apparent reason.

Some babies want more milk on days when they eat very little solid food, but others just seem to be less hungry altogether. A baby who asks for more milk feedings may be on a milk "fad" (see page 146) or just be in need of a bit of comfort. All of this is normal. What's important is not to let it worry you: mealtimes that are stressful for the parents are almost always stressful for the child too, and it is all too easy to let a simple appetite blip escalate into a battle of wills. A stressful meal won't be fun for any of you—and it won't help your baby's appetite, either!

It's important not to try to persuade your baby to eat by coaxing or forcing him. This will probably only make him confused and upset—and it could also risk creating an unhappy attitude toward food. Bear in mind that no baby or young child will starve himself intentionally—provided nourishing food is available they will always eat according to their needs, and if they miss a few days they'll make up for it when they need to.

What you can do:

- Offer your baby plenty of fluids. If you are breast-feeding, frequent breast-feeds may be enough; if you're formula-feeding, offer both water and formula.

- Continue to offer him small amounts of nutritious food at mealtimes.
- Make sure you are not overloading his plate—some babies will push away a big portion of food because it over-whelms them. Offer him just a little food and let him ask for more if he wants it.

My nine-month-old baby doesn't want to eat at the table, but he really loves foraging for crumbs and bits of food from the floor. Is this normal? Should I discourage it?

It's not unusual or abnormal for babies to enjoy picking up bits of food wherever they find them; it seems a fairly natural way to eat, and isn't that different from adults eating at a buffet or picnic—it's just that a baby will find the food that's on the floor because they crawl or shuffle everywhere. If you have a toddler as well it's almost inevitable your baby will come across a half-eaten apple or cracker at some point, and many parents find their baby has started solids "unofficially" by finding some tasty morsel left behind by an older brother or sister.

Exploring food by foraging may be a way of learning how to judge which foods are safe and which aren't (see also page 21). However, although there is a theory that babies need a certain amount of dirt to help to develop their immune systems, food that has been left lying around for a while, especially on the floor, may carry germs that can cause quite serious food poisoning, so eating this way shouldn't be encouraged.

Although your baby may just be exploring, it could also be that mealtimes aren't very enjoyable for him. If he doesn't enjoy eating at the table, the reason may be something as simple as not being very comfortable. Many high chairs are designed for toddlers and are too big for babies—the tray may be too high for him, or he may feel restricted or insecure in it.

Often babies are much happier sitting on their parent's lap for the first few weeks or months of solids, and enjoy picking up bits of food from someone else's plate.

It could be that your baby isn't enjoying mealtimes for some other reason. This can easily be the case if he is expected to sit quietly at the table for long periods, is eating alone, or isn't allowed the freedom to play with his food—maybe he has discovered that he can explore food on his own time and in his own way under the table, with no one "helping." Also, some babies can be turned off from their food if they are made to feel self-conscious or under pressure by their parents (or others) watching every mouthful they eat (see page 79). Having a picnic on a clean sheet or mat—either indoors or outdoors—can make change from sitting at the table for you both, and is a good way to help your baby to rediscover the fun of sharing mealtimes.

What you can do:

- Eat with your baby whenever possible.
- Make sure he is comfortable sitting at the table.
- Allow him to play with his food and make a mess when he's eating.
- Try not to stare at your baby while he's eating.
- Don't force him to sit at the table for long periods when he's lost interest in eating.
- Make sure there is no food left lying around on the floor or low surfaces.
- If your baby isn't enjoying being at the table, try having a picnic for a change of scenery.

My 10-month-old still isn't interested in solids. Is this a problem?

Although many babies are eager to get right into solid foods as soon as they are given the chance at six months, plenty of others aren't seriously interested until they are eight or nine months or even older. The current World Health Organization recommendation is that solids should be introduced *from* about six months old. But this doesn't mean that all babies will be ready at exactly that age—in the same way that not all babies will walk at one year.

At six months, breast milk and formula don't suddenly become inadequate as sources of nutrients; a baby's milk feedings can (and should) provide most of his nourishment for several more months, with just a few additions (see page 121). What matters is that the baby should have the chance to decide what else he needs.

Anecdotal evidence suggests that babies whose families have a history of allergy tend to be late starters with solids when they have the choice; this may be important for minimizing the chances of an allergic reaction while the baby is very young. Supplements of vitamins A, C, and D and iron may be particularly useful for these babies, but you may want to check with your pediatrician before administering vitamins to your child.

A very small number of babies have a physical condition (such as muscle weakness or an abnormality of their throat) that prevents them from developing normal self-feeding skills. It's possible that, in rare cases, such a condition will have remained unnoticed until the baby is over six months old. In this case, slowness to develop skills related to self-feeding may be the first sign that there is anything wrong. If you have any doubts about your baby's general development—for example, if he doesn't seem to be able to pick up his toys and take them to his mouth—then it would be a good idea to have him checked by a doctor, just in case his apparent lack of interest is actually part of a more serious problem.

What you can do:

- Avoid the temptation to describe your baby as a "poor eater" or to say that he has a "poor appetite." Provided you are still giving him as much breast milk (or formula) as he wants, he will be eating as much other food as he needs—there's nothing poor about that!
- Continue including your baby in mealtimes and letting him handle food, even if he doesn't seem interested. That way, he will begin to eat more as soon as he's ready.

My baby is seven months old. My mom is worried that all he does is play with his food. Is this a problem?

Trusting your baby to eat as much as he needs *and* allowing him to handle—or play with—his food are probably two of the most important elements of BLW. They are also the aspects of BLW that parents (and grandparents) find most difficult to adjust to. For generations parents were encouraged to make sure their babies finished every last bit of food, whether they wanted to or not. Making sure babies put on lots of weight was the goal, and playing with food was seen as wasteful, bad manners, and naughty.

We now know that putting on too much weight is bad for babies and that they actually need to eat very little in the first few months of starting solids. Breast milk or formula provides the nutrition and the calories; food provides an important learning experience, which will contribute to healthy eating in its own way, later.

Playing is your baby's main tool for learning about how things work and for developing new skills, so it's important to provide him with as many opportunities to play as possible. Squashing food, smearing it, and dropping it on the floor can teach your baby about volume, size, shape, and texture—and about different types of food, what they taste like, and how to handle them.

As your baby gets older he'll eat more and play less, but he will still need to play with his food sometimes. Allowing a baby the freedom to spend as long as he wants playing with food and not rushing him to eat ensures that his skills develop at the pace that's right for him (see Chapter 2). As his need for food increases, so do his self-feeding skills. Many parents who have followed BLW with their baby report that he is more skilled with his hands at, say, nine months old than their friends' babies of the same age, or than his spoon-fed brothers or sisters were at this age.

Handling food before he puts it in his mouth also helps your baby to work out how to deal with the food when it *is* in his mouth, so he is likely to be better than his peers at managing foods of different textures. And letting them play with food gives babies the skills to feed themselves a wide variety of foods, making them more likely to be well nourished.

Occasionally an older baby will play with his food because he is bored with that particular food—he may still be hungry, but wants (or needs) something new to eat. The easiest way to check is simply to offer him something different, or something from your plate.

Trusting your baby to eat enough can be difficult, especially in the beginning, but many parents and grandparents worry simply because their expectations of what the baby should be eating are unrealistic (see page 142).

In general, as long as your baby is able to use his hands to explore objects and is offered plenty of opportunities to handle a variety of healthy foods, you can rely on his instincts to eat as much as he needs. Until he is at least a year old breast milk or formula will be the mainstay of his nutrition. If he is wetting and filling his diapers and seems healthy and thriving then he's eating enough.

What you can do:

- Encourage your mother to talk about her concerns.
- Point out to her how well and happy your baby is and encourage her to see things from his point of view.
- Have faith in your convictions—time will show that your instinct to follow BLW is right, when your baby turns into a sociable, capable, and enthusiastic mealtime companion who *loves* his grandma's cooking!

"Once you accept that food is part of their entertainment, not a chore to get through, everything is so much more enjoyable."   *Joanne, mother of Caitlyn, 2*

Conclusion

WE HOPE YOU have enjoyed reading this book and that you and your baby are having healthy, happy mealtimes as a result.

We also hope that you've gained insight into why BLW is the logical way to introduce solids and how it fits perfectly with the natural development of babies' skills, as well as with the other things that they are learning in their first year. Baby-led weaning can help prevent the sorts of battles over food that are an all-too-common story among the parents of toddlers and young children, and it can contribute to making family mealtimes fun for everyone. In a nutshell, it makes eating the pleasure it should be.

Baby-led weaning makes perfect sense as a natural part of growing up. Not only does children's general development play a huge part in their ability to feed themselves, but what they learn through playing a full, active part in family meals has the potential to contribute to many different areas of their developing personality and skills.

There is a growing amount of evidence that the way children are fed when they are very young establishes the way they will feel about food throughout their childhood, and maybe even into adulthood. Obesity and eating disorders are in the news almost every week, and their consequences can be serious and distressing. Many of these problems have their roots in one (or both) of two key issues: appetite recognition and control. The healthy development of both of these things is at the heart of BLW.

So much of the advice parents are given about infant feeding is still based on the abilities of three- or four-month-old babies and the assumption that babies need to be spoon-fed. It rarely takes into account the natural abilities of six-month-old babies to take the lead with solids and feed themselves. Baby-led weaning brings together what we now know about when a baby should start solids with what we can see babies are able to do at this age.

We hope we've given you some practical ideas for how to go about using BLW with your own child, how to make it safe and enjoyable, and what to expect as your baby's skills progress.

Finally, we'd like to thank all the parents who have contributed their firsthand knowledge to help us write this book. We hope that their experiences of sharing their baby's joy and wonder at discovering food have inspired you as much as they inspired us. It's their stories, above all else, that show that BLW simply makes sense.

Appendix 1: The Story of Baby-Led Weaning

Although the practice of BLW has probably always existed, the theory of why and how it works was developed by *Baby-Led Weaning* coauthor Gill Rapley.[1] As a public health nurse for more than 20 years she encountered many families who were experiencing problems feeding their babies; many babies resisted being spoon-fed or would accept only a very limited number of foods. Some parents had resorted to force-feeding in an effort to get their children to eat. Choking and gagging on lumpy meals was common. Mealtimes were extremely stressful for both the parents and their babies.

Gill suspected that the babies were resisting *what was being done to them* rather than the food itself. The simple suggestion to wait a bit longer (if the baby was under six months), or to let the baby have a go himself (if he was older), seemed to make a huge difference, both to the babies' behavior and to the parents' stress levels. It all boiled down to giving control back to the baby—which raised the question "Why did we take it away in the first place?"

As part of her master's degree,[2] Gill recruited a small group of parents, with babies of four months old (the minimum recommended age for solids at the time), to help her observe what the babies would do if they were offered the chance to touch and handle food without being spoon-fed. The babies were all fully breast-feeding at the start of the study, and they continued to be breast-fed throughout. The study ended when they reached nine months.

The parents were asked to sit their baby with them at mealtimes and to allow him to handle and explore different foods and, if he wanted, to eat them. The parents made short films of the babies' behavior at mealtimes every two weeks and completed a diary of their responses to food and their general development.

The films and diaries showed that, at four months, the babies were not able to pick food up but that they began to reach out for it soon after that. Once they started grabbing it (some earlier than others), they all took it to their mouths. Some gnawed or munched on the food from as early as five months, but they didn't swallow any of it. They all appeared completely absorbed in what they were doing, even though they didn't need to eat the food.

By about six and a half months almost all the babies seemed to have worked out how to get food to their mouths and, after apparently "practicing" chewing for a week or two, they were beginning to find out how to swallow it. Gradually they began to "play" less with the food and their eating became more purposeful. As their hand-eye coordination and fine motor skills developed, they were able to pick up smaller and smaller pieces.

By nine months all the babies were eating a wide range of normal family foods. Most used their fingers, but some were beginning to manage spoons or forks. Their parents reported that they had no difficulties with lumps, and they hardly ever gagged while eating. The babies were all willing to try new foods, and they seemed to enjoy mealtimes.

At around the same time that Gill was conducting her study, a great deal of research was emerging to show that, ideally, babies should have nothing but breast milk until they are six months old, and that they should move gradually toward a mixed diet after that. Gill's findings, together with the many parents' stories that support them, suggest that normal healthy human babies—like infant mammals everywhere—develop the skills they need to feed themselves with solid foods at just the right age.

Appendix 2: Basic Rules for Food Safety

Bacteria can spread and multiply quickly in food, and babies are more at risk than adults of becoming ill through food poisoning. Chemicals can also get into food and cause illness. To keep your family safe, it's best to follow these simple rules:

1. You (and your family)

Wash your hands with soap and rinse them thoroughly:
- before handling food
- between the handling of raw and ready-to-eat foods
- after touching the trash bin
- after touching your face or hair
- after handling cleaning materials
- after touching pets or their bedding or food bowls
- after using the bathroom
- Take particular care with hand-washing if you have a cold or a flu bug.

- Wash your baby's hands with mild soap and water before offering her food, and encourage other members of the family to wash their hands before sitting down to a meal.

2. Surfaces and equipment

- Clean all surfaces and equipment thoroughly before and after you prepare food and after they have been used with raw food.
- Clean cutting boards and knives thoroughly after using them for raw food. If possible, have two different boards and keep one for raw food and one for ready-to-eat food.

3. Storage of food

- Follow storage instructions given on food packages.
- Put foods that have a "use by" date (as opposed to just a "best before" date) into the fridge as soon as possible after you get them home.
- Return chilled and frozen foods to the fridge or freezer as soon as possible after use.
- Check frequently that stored food is not out of date. Confirm before using it that any food near its "use by" date is not already going bad.
- Wrap or cover all raw or uncooked foods, especially meat and fish, and store them in the bottom of the fridge so that they can't touch or drip on to other foods.
- Food that is not to be eaten hot should be covered, cooled quickly and put into the fridge or freezer as soon as it is cold. This is especially important for meat, fish, eggs, and rice, all of which can contain germs that multiply rapidly at room temperature. (Food will cool faster in small amounts and in shallow dishes than in large quantities. Rice can be rinsed in cold water to cool it quickly.)

- Invest in a fridge thermometer. Keep it in the coldest part of the fridge (usually in the back at the bottom) and check the temperature regularly. Aim to keep the temperature between 0°C and 5°C (32°F and 41°F). If the temperature is higher, remember that the food will not keep for as long. To keep food at the right temperature in the fridge:

  - don't leave the fridge door open longer than absolutely necessary
  - don't put foods that expire quickly in the door of the fridge
  - don't put hot food into the fridge as this will raise the temperature of the whole fridge
  - There is a theory that the acid in fruit and vegetables can react with the metal in tin (aluminum) foil, releasing chemicals into the food. It may be best not to use foil to wrap these foods.
  - If you use plastic wrap, check that it is of a type that is safe to use with food. If in doubt, put the food in a bowl and cover the bowl with the film so that it doesn't touch the food itself.
  - Check the manufacturer's instructions for storage times for frozen foods.

4. Cooking food

- Wash fruit and vegetables thoroughly and rinse meat, poultry, fish, and rice before cooking.
- Thaw frozen meat and poultry thoroughly before cooking. It's safer to defrost it slowly in the fridge or quickly, by microwaving, than to leave it sitting at room temperature.
- Make sure that food is thoroughly cooked. Before serving, check that it's piping hot all the way through and that

meat juices run clear. Don't shorten cooking times given on package labels or in cookbooks.

- Use the recommended oven temperature for oven-cooked foods, and follow the instructions carefully if using a microwave.
- Ensure that eggs are always thoroughly cooked. Avoid recipes that include eggs which won't be cooked, such as mayonnaise.
- If possible, serve food as soon as it is cooked. If you need to keep it hot, make sure that it stays above 63°C (145°F). If you can't keep it that hot it should be used within two hours, or chilled and put into the fridge for reheating later. This is especially important for meat, fish, eggs, and rice.
- Chilled, cooked food should be reheated once only. Make sure it is piping hot all the way through before serving.

References

Chapter 1: What is Baby-Led Weaning?

1. *The Compact Oxford English Dictionary*, 3rd edn (Oxford University Press, 2005).

2. *The American Heritage Dictionary of the English Language*, 4th edn (Houghton Mifflin, 2000).

3. WHO/UNICEF, *Global Strategy for Infant and Young Child Feeding* (WHO, Geneva, 2002).

4. World Health Organization Web site: www.who.int/childgrowth/standards/weight_for_age/en/.

5. World Health Organization, *International Code of Marketing of Breast-milk Substitutes* (WHO, Geneva, 1981).

Chapter 2: How Does Baby-Led Weaning Work?

1. C. M. Davis, "Self-selection of diet by newly weaned infants: an experimental study," *American Journal of Diseases in Childhood*, 36: 4 (1928), 651–79.

Chapter 5: After the Early Days

1. Work of Professor Malcolm Povey, http://www.food.leeds.ac.uk/mp.htm.

Appendix 1: The Story of Baby-Led Weaning

1. G. Rapley (V. H. Moran and F. Dykes, eds.), *Baby-Led Weaning* in *Maternal and Infant Nutrition and Nurture: Controversies and Challenges* (London, Quay Books, 2006).

2. G. Rapley, "Can babies initiate and direct the weaning process?" Unpublished MSc, Interprofessional Health and Community Studies (Canterbury Christ Church University, Kent, 2003).

Photo Credits

(All page numbers below refer to the photo insert.)

Page 1
Photo 1: Chris Carden
Photo 2: Nick Jones
Photo 4: Anna Bird

Page 2
Photo 1: Janice Milnerwood
Photo 2: Shaun Murkett
Photo 3: Tracey Murkett
Photo 4: John Johnston

Page 3
Photo 1: Samantha Jones
Photo 2: Shaun Murkett
Photo 3: Je-Mai Chisholm
Photo 4: Amber Rowland

Page 4
Photo 2: Natalie Blechner

Page 5
Photo 1: Cate Garratt
Photo 2: Emma Brown
Photo 3: Tracey Murkett

Page 6
Photo 1: Fred Coster
Photo 2: Fred Coster
Photo 3: Natalie Blechner
Photo 4: Amber Rowland

Page 7
Photo 1: Jason Woolfe
Photo 2: Jason Woolfe
Photo 3: Gladys Perrier (of
    Perrier Pictures)

Page 8
Photo 1: Jane Kellas
Photo 2: Samantha Jones
Photo 3: Tracey Murkett
Photo 4: Tracey Murkett

Acknowledgments

WE WOULD LIKE to thank everyone who contributed their ideas, experiences, comments, and wisdom to make this book possible. We are particularly grateful to Jessica Figueras, Hazel Jones, Derrick Murkett, Sam Padain, Gabrielle Palmer, Magda Sachs, Mary Smale, Alison Spiro, Sarah Squires, and Carol Williams for valuable feedback on the manuscript and for insight, support, and inspiration.

Special thanks go to the many parents who sent us photos of their babies' adventures with food—we wish we could have included them all.

Thanks, also, to our editor Julia Kellaway for her patience and tolerance.

Finally, we would like to thank our families for their constant support while we were writing, from reading the manuscript and IT help to photography, babysitting, and making the tea. Our partners, in particular, deserve a medal.

This book is for our children, who continue to teach us so much.

Index

INDEX

digestion and nutrition issues,
54–56
preparation of, 26
wasted food with, 203

rashes, 102
readiness for solid foods
false signs of, 6–8, 56, 59
true signs of, 8–9
real food, experience of, 25
rejecting food, 74
restaurants, 27–28, 165–169
rewards, 171–173
rice, 112
rice cereal, 59, 124
rules of adult eating, 137–138
runny foods, 137–138

safe eating
basic rules for, 223–226
gag reflex and, 46–47, 76–77
learning about, 21
snacking and, 155
salt, 97–99
scheduling meals, 63–66
self-consciousness, 79
self-service, 169–171
serving themselves (toddlers),
169–171
shape of food, 66–67
silverware, 137, 158–161
sippy cups, 162
size of a baby, 7–8, 10
skills, feeding-related
coordination, 67–69
hand skills and, 22, 32, 49, 66–67
mouth skills, 32–34
order of development, 31
swallowing, 34
skin on fruits and vegetables,
107–108
sleep, 7, 59
small children. *See* toddlers
snacks, 117, 154–155, 170
sodium, 99

soluble fiber, 194–195
soup, 137, 138
spices and herbs, 132
spicy foods, 133–134
spinach, 197
spitting out, 18, 19, 132
splash mats, 86, 169
Spock, Benjamin, 52
spoon-feeding. *See also* puréed or
mashed food
appetite control and, 45
cereals and, 125
changing to BLW, 92–94
combining BLW with, 200–202
gagging and, 47
games and tricks in, 2, 27, 54
as interruption of self-feeding, 37
myths about necessity of, 200–201
as "normal," 2–3
playing at, 161
problems with, 14–19
speed of, 60–61
tongue thrust and, 42
"window of opportunity" and, 44
spoons, learning to use, 137, 159–161
starch, 125, 187, 192–193
stool and bowel movements, 55,
139–141, 209–211
storing food safely, 224–225
strawberries, 102
straws, 168
stress, 212
sugar, 99–100, 192–193
suspicion of food, 23
swallowing, 34, 38
sweet foods, 99–100, 118–119,
171–173

tablecloths, 86, 90
table manners, 137–138, 158,
163–165
taste preferences and BLW, 20–21
tastes and flavors, 131–134
tea, 101, 150, 197
teeth, 43

About the Authors

Gill Rapley has studied infant feeding and child development for many years. She worked as a public health nurse for more than 20 years and has also been a midwife and a breast-feeding counselor. She developed the theory of baby-led weaning while studying babies' developmental readiness for solids as part of her master's degree. She lives in Kent, England, with her husband and has three grown children, all of whom tried their best to show her that they didn't need any help with solid foods.

Tracey Murkett is a freelance writer and journalist. After following baby-led weaning with her daughter, she wanted to let other parents know how easy and stress-free mealtimes with babies and young children can be. She lives in London with her partner and their five-year-old daughter.

They are also the authors of *The Baby-Led Weaning Cookbook: 130 Easy, Nutritious Recipes That Will Help Your Baby Learn to Eat (and Love!) a Variety of Solid Foods—and That the Whole Family Will Enjoy.*